Lovely
lace
knits

gabrielle vézina

CREATOR OF GABRIELLE KNITS

Lovely
lace
knits

LEARN THE ART OF
LACEWORK WITH
16 Timeless Patterns

PAGE STREET
PUBLISHING CO.

PAGE STREET
PUBLISHING CO.

Copyright © 2023

First published in 2023 by Gabrielle Vézina

Page Street Publishing Co.

27 Congress Street, Suite 1511

Salem, MA 01970

www.pagestreetpublishing.com

Distributed by Macmillan, sales in Canada by The Canadian Manda Group.

27 26 25 24 23 1 2 3 4 5

ISBN-13: 978-1-64567-732-1
ISBN-10: 1-64567-732-X

Library of Congress Control Number: 2022945420

Cover and book design by Laura Benton for Page Street Publishing Co.
Photography by Robert Tétreault

Printed and bound in the United States

Dedication

To my mother, Loraine, who taught me that knitting books are meant to bring joy.

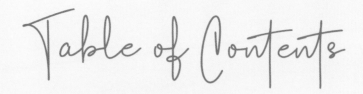
Table of Contents

Introduction

Creating Beauty in a Fast World

I knit and wear knitted garments and accessories all year long. It's in line with my desire to live slowly and beautifully in a world in which everything goes too fast. I do my best to take the time to stop, observe, breathe and laugh. Creating beauty a stitch at a time is one of the ways I fight the urge to always be as productive as possible. It forces me to relax and enjoy the moment and the small movements of my hands; it helps me to accept the fact that not everything can be, should be or needs to be made quickly. Savoring the gradual process and being rewarded with a result that has no equivalent in the fast-fashion world is greatly fulfilling.

I find inspiration in the beauty around me. I live in a city where concrete and flowers coexist unexpectedly but peacefully. This union makes sense, creating an amalgam of impressive man-made constructions and omnipresent natural wonders. Those wonders are as big as a mountain in the middle of the city and as small as the prettiest rocks that my kids find in their urban explorations. I try to look through their eyes to see beauty in an ordinary pebble. It's not always easy. When we grow up, we often lose the ability to be amazed by the small things. Yet this ability is still in each of us, hidden under a mile-long to-do list. When I manage to let go of all my adult concerns (after all, do they really matter that much?), I let my kids show me the way. We stop and watch the birds. We marvel at the leaf-covered sidewalk. We put out our tongues and catch snowflakes. And when we come home, I sit down and write knitting patterns, my head filled with these simple beauties.

When I was a kid, my mother was a seamstress and a fashion design teacher. We lived in apartments that were so small she had to sleep in the living room—but we always had a sewing room. As far back as I can remember, my whole wardrobe was handmade. I picked the yarn or the fabric, and we planned the pattern together. My mother taught me pretty much everything I know, though she says that she didn't teach me anything. Every time she tried, I replied that I already knew. And I was right!

The truth is that I was observing her, listening carefully while she narrated the lesson that she would teach the next day, whether it was about sleeves, necklines, grading or patternmaking. And even if I am a very bad seamstress, my mother's teachings weren't lost on me. When I finally jumped into knitting after spending my teenage years sewing and crocheting my wardrobe, it all fell into place. I've always been enthusiastic about everything arts and crafts; I've been conceiving my own clothes for my whole life; and as a former programmer, making sense out of numbers is one of my passions.

Designing knitting patterns is the perfect blend of everything I love. I started in my twenties, and my fascination has continued to grow with time. I've learned a lot of techniques over the years, and I make it a point to learn new ones on a regular basis. Knitting is an incredibly vast field of expertise that I explore with the same amazement that I see in my kids' eyes when a shiny, colorful pebble crosses their paths. Since 2012, I have designed more than 100 patterns of all kinds, involving several techniques: all sorts of colorwork (especially stranded and mosaic), cables, 3D knitting, thrumming, various textures and, of course, lace. Coming up with new lace stitch patterns—as well as modifying and combining patterns from stitch pattern books—has become second nature to me. Over the years, I have developed a deep understanding of how stitches work together and how they can blend gracefully within the specific shape of a garment.

Lace knitting is my favorite technique for making beautiful creations with my hands. I call out the stitches in my head as if it they were a mantra or a nursery rhyme. It soothes me. And it amazes me with every row to see that each movement of my hands has a meaning: Each one creates a tiny part of the beautiful larger piece that I'm making. Each stitch is a drop in the ocean, a second in a day, a step in the creation of something meaningful.

I also find great pleasure in grading garments. As a geeky person obsessed with numbers and spreadsheets, I am very interested in understanding the math behind different body shapes. I study with care all the standard and newly made size charts, and I review my numbers with every new design to make sure that they will fit everyone who wants to knit them. They aren't tailored, but I want them to be flattering on all kinds of bodies. Uniqueness in body shapes is what makes the world beautiful, like a landscape composed of many different elements. Handmade patterns should enhance everyone's beauty and embrace diversity.

My designs are meant for day-to-day wearing, with coziness and elegance in mind. Comfort and warmth are the basis of the simple and enjoyable lifestyle that I'm aiming for. At the same time, elegance is also an important factor in my designs: I enjoy feminine garments, dainty looks and the originality that homemade knitted pieces are sure to bring.

This book features four collections of knitted patterns. The pieces created in each collection can be worn together for an everything-is-knitted look or separately to get your daily dose of knitwear. They are simple enough to find their place in a day-to-day wardrobe, and hopefully they are timeless enough to be part of a sustainable, long-lasting collection of clothes. Some of them are small and can be completed quickly, while others are large with intricate patterns and will take some time to finish. I encourage you to knit them in a color palette that makes you feel at ease and to use fibers that you will enjoy with every stitch and every time you wear them.

Most of all, I hope this book will bring you joy and serenity, both in the process of knitting these designs and while you are wearing the finished pieces. I also hope that this book will make you proud of your craft and that these pieces will make you feel as beautiful as you are.

Gabrielle Vézina

What Is Lace Knitting?

Lace knitting is a classical technique that became extremely popular in the occidental world in the 1800s. Two centuries later, it hasn't lost its shine. It is a staple in both the art of knitting and the clothes that we buy. Lace is everywhere: frilly hems, dainty tops, summer dresses and even charming underwear. We perceive lace as a feminine addition to any fabric. It adds frivolity, grace and delicacy. Using lace in knitting is a sure way to create an intricate-looking fabric and add interest to any basic garment.

The main characteristic of lace knitting is the holes made in the fabric, usually created by making yarn overs. Yarn overs create new stitches that need to be paired with decreases to make the stitch count even. While yarn overs are nothing but holes in the knit fabric, decreases can be made in several ways. They can be left- or right-leaning or in the middle; in addition, they can decrease only one stitch or can be used to balance several yarn overs.

Other interesting components are often added to lace patterns: bobbles (my favorites!), invisible increases, slip stitches, twisted stitches and other less common stitches that add a touch of originality to your knitted pieces.

Lace patterns can be as simple as performing (yo, k2tog) every few stitches to create eyelets, or they can be as complex as a full yoke made of a lace pattern that is different at every row, like the Amarelle Sweater (page 85). In general, lace patterns are repeated several times over the garment, no matter if the whole stitch pattern is made over only a few rows—like only four rows, as in the Samara Cardigan (page 57)—or a much longer repeat, like 24 rows, as in the Solstice Top (page 123).

The art of creating an interesting lace pattern relies on the way the yarn overs, decreases and other embellishing stitches are arranged together in a cohesive and pleasing way. Some experts say that "real" lace must have lace stitches in all rows, even on the wrong side. I am more liberal in my interpretation of lace knitting: I think that any pattern that is pleasing to the human eye and incorporates yarn overs as a design element can be called lace.

In a garment or an accessory, lace can be integrated in several ways. It can be the only design element and be used over the whole piece, as in the Winter Wheat Scarf (page 67). It can be used to enhance a garment made in classical stockinette or garter stitch by adding texture to only a part of the garment, such as the sleeves, hem, yoke and so on. Lace patterns can be combined together, moving from one to the other in a graceful way, as in the Harvest Moon Shawl (page 33), which uses four different patterns to create a unique design. No matter which pattern you choose to make first, you will soon discover the beauty of lace and how it can add interest and intrigue to any project you make.

While it may not be as crucial in other forms of knitting, blocking is an essential step in lace knitting. Sometimes this can be achieved by simply washing and laying the piece flat to dry. Other times, especially when working with lighter yarns, the piece has to be carefully stretched out and pinned down on a blocking mat. In all cases, the magic happens when this step is completed. The lace stitches will then bloom and reveal their true beauty. After blocking, you'll finally be able to reap the rewards of your work. (For more information on blocking, see page 15.)

Lace Knitting

Essential Tips and Tricks

Knitting lace is a skill that beginning knitters often perceive as intimidating, because it looks so intricate. However, I'm sure that it will become one of your favorite techniques with just a bit of practice! Lace can be complicated, that's for sure, but it also can be extremely simple—and, regardless of its complexity, it always creates impressive results. Another boon of lace knitting is that it requires only one strand of yarn. Lacework patterns also use mostly basic stitches and are usually repetitive, which allows you to memorize the pattern and find a soothing knitting pace. Even if you have yet to learn some of the stitches used in a pattern, most of them are easy to perform with a little practice. Here, I'll share a few general tips to ease your lace knitting journey in the hope that it will be a pleasant one.

What Yarn Should Be Used to Knit Lace?

The short answer is that any yarn will work, as long as it feels good in your hands. I'd recommend avoiding two characteristics: (1) Your yarn shouldn't be splitty, and (2) it shouldn't be too fuzzy. Other than those two qualifiers, you can use any yarn that inspires you to knit.

Though lace projects are often worked with thin or lightweight yarns, they can be made with any yarn weight and still give stunning results. With thin yarns, several rows and stitches will cover only a small area, allowing you to work an intricate pattern with both subtlety and complexity. With thicker yarns, the texture is less subtle and is sure to make a statement with the big holes made from the yarn overs. I especially enjoy working my lace projects with a range of yarns from light fingering to double knit (DK) weight, and I occasionally pick a beautiful laceweight yarn or a worsted weight that works up in no time. In all cases, your yarn must be easy to knit with and easy to unravel in case you ever need to. You should avoid loosely plied yarns or any yarn that tends to be splitty. Single-ply or tightly plied yarns are easier to use.

Regarding the fiber choice, I prefer animal-based fibers that have more elasticity than plant-based yarns and synthetic fibers. This elasticity makes knitting lace easier and makes the yarn more forgiving if some stitches are uneven, which make these yarns a good choice for beginners—and everyone! For knitters with some experience (and for motivated beginners as well), linen, cotton, silk, bamboo and others are sure to give a chic texture to your lace project. They are a great fit for lighter garments that are a delight to wear during summertime. Acrylic also has appeal with its softness, warmth and easy care, which make it perfect for warm hats and projects for children.

I adore working with fuzzy yarns, as you can see in the *Hazy Collection* (page 54). However, I avoid knitting lace with extremely hairy fibers, such as Suri or mohair worked alone, as the patterns are harder to decrypt when they are buried in hair. For my fuzzy projects, I like to use yarns made from alpaca, llama and untreated hairy sheep breeds or a strand of mohair worked with a strand of smoother yarn.

What Are the Best Needles to Use?

This question is very personal and so is the answer. What feels good between your hands, gives you a nice tension and makes you happy is your best bet. In general, you should favor needles with sharp tips. They can easily pick up tiny strands of yarn, even when you need to pick three stitches at once.

When taking the material into consideration, you should know that smooth needles—such as aluminum, stainless steel or carbon—are easy to work with. They are slick, which allows the stitches to move freely and helps you knit faster. Wooden needles have a better grip: The stitches won't fall as easily on wood, which can be an advantage for beginners.

When using circular needles, make sure to pick needles that have a smooth join between the needle and the cord, as thinner yarn can get caught in the junction. Interchangeable sets are incredibly versatile, but this is their weak spot, especially when you use the smallest needles of the set. For this reason, I enjoy working with fixed circular needles when knitting lace.

Playing It Safe: Lifelines, Stitch Markers and Counting Stitches

Nothing is worse than spotting a mistake in your knitting ten rows back and having to unravel all that hard work, or finding that your stitch count doesn't correspond to what you should have . . . without knowing what went wrong. Following are some tips that can help you avoid those unpleasant situations.

LIFELINES

You can add lifelines to your work when you don't feel confident or when you suspect that the next part of the pattern will be tricky. To do so, use a strand of spare yarn—ideally one that is thinner than your working yarn—and use a tapestry needle to thread it through all the stitches of the current row. Take note of the row where your lifeline is placed and keep knitting the project. If you make a mistake that you're unable to correct, remove your needle, unravel all the stitches until you reach the lifeline, place this row's stitches back on your needle and start that part of the pattern again. But if all is fine and you're happy with your work, hooray! You can simply pull on the lifeline to remove it and place another one a few rows farther on in the project if you feel like you need it.

STITCH MARKERS

Stitch markers help you recognize certain specific spots, such as the beginning of a round or the location to enclose a stitch pattern. The number of stitch markers recommended is kept minimal throughout this book. However, there is nothing preventing you from adding more. For example, when a lace pattern is repeated several times in a row, such as in the Amarelle Sweater (page 85), you can add a marker at each repetition. This way, when you slip a marker, you'll know it's time to start reading the chart back at the first stitch. Keep in mind that the markers stated in the pattern should be recognizable, so using different colors or designs of stitch markers is useful when you add more than the recommended number.

COUNTING STITCHES

Counting stitches after each row is probably the simplest yet safest way to avoid having to unravel several rows. In the patterns of this book, the number of stitches you should have is stated each time this number changes or after completing a chart. Refer to the stitch count of the pattern. If you have the same number of stitches, good! If you don't, try finding where the error lies and correct it or unravel until your work seems correct.

Correcting Mistakes

Repairing lace can be tricky. All the decreases can make the operation very confusing, and if you can't find exactly where the error is, undoing a part of your work is often the way to go. But sometimes you can save your work. The most common error is a dropped yarn over. Fortunately, this is easy to repair! If you have a dropped yarn over on the previous row, you can simply use your left-hand needle to pick up the bar between the stitches where the yarn over was supposed to be and work it as you would have worked the yarn over. If it was a few rows before and no lace stitches were worked in these rows, you can pick up the bar at the row where the yarn over should be and re-create the stitches of the following rows by passing each bar over the next row's bar (this will create knit stitches). With some practice, you'll find that you can correct decreases by unraveling a few stitches on a few rows and reworking the lace pattern using the loose strands that you'll have. It's not easy, but it can be worth trying if you're about to unravel!

Sometimes the mistakes are small, subtle and hard to repair, but you can see a way of fixing the stitch count without completely ruining the pattern and without unraveling. If you're hesitating between unraveling or using a quick fix that will leave a mistake in your work, ask yourself these questions: Will it be visible enough that people will notice the mistake, or will you be the only one to know? Will the quick fix bother you forever and stop you from wearing the garment? Is the idea of unraveling so demotivating that you'll just put the project into a dusty pile of unfinished projects? Do what feels best for you. Most important of all, don't become discouraged over small imperfections—a lot of my projects have small, unnoticeable errors. After all, aren't those small mistakes just a part of the beauty of handmade pieces?

Basic Lace Stitches

THE YARN OVER STITCH

Yarn overs (yo) are the very foundation of lacework and they are, of all existing stitches, the easiest ones to perform. Any beginner can learn to work a yarn over, as it simply means to wrap the yarn over the needle, thus creating a new stitch. That's why basic lace is a beginner-friendly technique.

To perform a yarn over, work your way up to the spot where you need to do the yarn over, bring the yarn to the front of your work, then wrap it over the right needle so the yarn is now on the back. If you need to knit the next stitch, keep the yarn on the back and knit as usual. If you need to purl the next stitch, bring the yarn to the front by passing it under the needle, and you're ready to purl. As long as you know one way to decrease a stitch to compensate for the yarn over, you can knit lace!

DECREASES: THE KEY TO A LOVELY PATTERN

Decreases are harder to perform than yarn overs, but they are crucial to shaping the lace pattern, as they give a direction to the stitches around the yarn overs. Therefore, you need to carefully work your decreases if you want the pattern to look right. What differentiates decreases is the way they are leaning: right, left or straight.

- **Right-leaning decreases** are usually made by knitting two stitches together (k2tog), the same way you would knit one stitch. You can perform more decreases in one stitch by knitting more stitches together at once (k3tog, k4tog and so on).

- **Left-leaning decreases** can be made in two different ways: (1) slip, slip, knit (ssk), or (2) slip, knit, pass the slipped stitch over (skp). In this book, I used slip, slip, knit, but the two are interchangeable. You can also perform more decreases by working more stitches together. For example, slip, slip, slip, knit (sssk) is often used in this book.

- **Straight decreases** are made by using the central double decrease (cdd). These decreases create lovely results when placed between two yarn overs, as they look like a vertical bar. They are made this way: Slip two stitches together knitwise, knit one, pass slipped stitches over. The same stitch is sometimes called by its long name: slip two, knit one, pass two over (s2kp), but it is referred to as "cdd" all throughout this book.

When decreases are worked on the wrong side of the piece, they are made the same way but by purling instead of knitting if working in a stockinette-based fabric. Their direction must be reversed in order to look correct on the right side of the work. But you don't have to worry about that, as it's always indicated in the pattern.

Blocking Your Lacework

I would like to reiterate the importance of blocking your work. A lace fabric will truly shine when it has been properly washed and blocked. The fibers relax in the water, and yarn overs tend to grow significantly after their first bath. You can use warm water with a soft soap when hand-washing your projects, as long as the water isn't too warm for your hands. The warmth accentuates the relaxing process. Simply move the project in the bath, smoothly, until it has completely softened. Once it is clean, use blocking mats or a carpet covered with a clean towel to lay your knit flat. Place it carefully, making sure that all dimensions are correct and that your knit isn't weirdly stretched out or sporting uneven edges. You can use regular pins, T-pins or knit blockers to secure your project. Let it dry completely before removing it.

Garments and accessories, such as socks and hats, need to be blocked to specific dimensions to make sure that the fit is right. However, for accessories like shawls and scarves, the blocking step should be used to emphasize the beauty of the lacework. Stretching the fabric a little more than usual is a good way to do so. When pinning your work, make sure that the edges aren't stretched out if they need to be even, like the Winter Wheat Scarf (page 67). On the other hand, you can create a lovely scalloped edge on the bottom of a shawl—like the Soft Breeze Shawl (page 132), for example—by stretching specific spots of each repetition of the lace pattern and pinning them in place.

Gauge and Yarn Weight Considerations

The Basics of a Gauge Swatch

We hear it all the time: Gauge is crucial. Well, I won't contradict that fact!

Gauge is the key to achieving a specific size. If you wish to achieve 40 inches (102 cm) at the bust, and the gauge is 20 stitches for 4 inches (10 cm), 200 stitches at the bust will give you exactly those 40 inches (102 cm). If the gauge is 32 stitches for 4 inches (10 cm), you will need 320 stitches at the bust to get the same measurements. That's a big difference! But you don't have to worry—the beauty of following a pattern is that the math has been taken care of for you. Your job is simply to get the correct gauge, follow the pattern and you'll get the correct size!

To be sure that your gauge is correct, you need to knit your swatch exactly the way you'll work your project. You need to use the same yarn and the same needles and work the swatch in the specified stitch pattern. If the project is worked in the round, you should also knit your swatch in the round. The bigger the swatch, the more accurate it will be. Also, be sure to block the swatch before measuring it, as all the measurements given in the book are the ones of a blocked project.

You can measure a gauge swatch in two ways. The first way is to knit a generous number of stitches to create a swatch larger than 4 inches (10 cm). After blocking your swatch, you can place a ruler in the middle of your work and count the number of stitches and rows comprised into 4 inches (10 cm). I favor this method for regular patterns, such as stockinette or garter stitch. The second way is to knit a specific number of stitches. You can use the number of stitches for 4 inches (10 cm) and add a few more stitches on the edges that you'll work in garter stitch (knit the stitches on all rows). Once your swatch is all done and blocked, measure it—hopefully, the pattern comprised within the edges of the swatch will have the correct measurements. I recommend using this second method for gauging lace patterns, as they are irregular and their stitches can be tricky to count.

If your swatch has a bigger gauge than the requirements, for example, if the required gauge is 20 stitches for 4 inches (10 cm) and you get 18 stitches for 4 inches (10 cm), using a smaller needle size will help you reach the correct gauge. Accordingly, a swatch with a smaller gauge (a greater number of stitches than the one specified) should be remade using a larger needle size.

With all that being said, sometimes the only way to achieve the specified gauge is to use a different yarn. Yarn weight and needle sizes are specified in the patterns, but those are indications only. You should be using what feels right for you and what allows you to achieve the correct gauge while creating a pleasing fabric.

Working with a Different Gauge

I think that handmade projects should be made to the knitter's liking and not solely the way that the designer planned the pattern. Actually, I especially enjoy seeing how knitters modify and interpret my patterns to make their own creations. For intermediate and advanced knitters, patterns are easy to modify in order to make them fit or to accommodate differences in yarn or available yardage. Of course, garments and accessories like hats and socks need to fit the wearer's measurements, and achieving the correct gauge is especially useful in these cases. On the other hand, shawls and scarves don't have a specific required size and can be made with various gauges and yarn weights. I encourage you to play with yarns and to pick what appeals to you. Keep in mind that if you're using a different yarn weight, the required quantity of yarn will differ. As a rule of thumb, you'll need more skeins of bigger yarn to achieve the same measurements.

You can also use a different gauge on garments. Even if your gauge is only slightly different, the measurements of your garment will be different. For example, if your gauge is 19 stitches instead of the suggested 20 stitches, having 200 stitches at the bust will result in a 42-inch (107-cm) sweater instead of 40 inches (102 cm). It may not seem like a huge difference, but it can be significant. If you feel good about the idea of having a few inches of difference, you can knit your normal size at a slightly different gauge and the result should be fine.

If you want to use a vastly different gauge, you will need to do some math to ensure the correct fit. Measure your bust, add the desired ease (a recommended ease is specified in each pattern) and use your swatch measurements to calculate how many stitches you'll need. Here are a few formulas for determining your new gauge:

bust measurement + ease = total bust size

swatch measurement for 4 inches (number of stitches) / 4 = stitches per inch

total bust size × stitches per inch = desired number of stitches at bust

You will then need to pick a size that has a number of stitches at the bust that is as close as possible to that number.

Since all the garment patterns of this book are worked from the top down, the number of stitches at the bust are indicated after separating the sleeve stitches and the body stitches—for example, the Pine Cone Sweater (page 23), Samara Cardigan (page 57) and Amarelle Sweater (page 85)—or after joining the back and front pieces together, like the Pinnate Tank Top (page 97) or Solstice Top (page 123). Look out for the "live stitch count at bust" indication. Also, because of the top-down construction, row gauge matters only on the top part. It isn't really an issue on the body or sleeves: You can work your garment to your desired length without worrying about working a specific number of rows.

Please note that the sleeve measurements will also vary according to your new gauge. The top arm measurements are relatively proportionate to the bust measurements, but if you're using a very different gauge than the specified one, you may want to look at the upper sleeve circumference measurement to make sure that the fit will be good.

The same goes for accessories that need to be made to a specific size, such as socks and hats. If your gauge differs from the one specified in the pattern, you can make sure that it will fit by using similar formulas:

swatch measurement for 4 inches (number of stitches) / 4 = stitches per inch

number of stitches stated in the pattern / stitches per inch = measurement in inches of the resulting project made at that gauge

In a pattern like the Woodland Socks (page 48), which has only one size, you can also reverse the formula to know what would be the required gauge to achieve your desired measurements. For example, if you want to achieve a leg circumference of 8.5 inches (21.5 cm) instead of the 8 inches (20.25 cm) that you'd have if you knit the pattern at the stated gauge, here's how to know at what gauge you should be knitting:

number of stitches in the pattern / desired final measurement = desired number of stitches per inch

desired number of stitches per inch × 4 = target swatch measurement for 4 inches (number of stitches)

In my example, you'll have:

48 stitches at leg circumference / 8.5 inches ≈ 5.65

5.65 × 4 = 22.6 stitches in 4 inches (10 cm)

If you achieve a gauge of 22.6 stitches instead of the 24 stitches stated in the pattern, you'll get your desired circumference of 8.5 inches (21.5 cm). Note that you can round the target gauge swatch to 22 or 23 stitches; the small difference in size will be easily corrected at the blocking step.

Other Modifications

Most patterns in this book, especially garments and neckwear, have constructions made to be adaptable in sizes. All garments are worked from the top down, which means that you can make them longer or shorter or work a different sleeve length. On the Amarelle Sweater (page 85), you can even make a different kind of cowl, as it is worked after the sweater is finished. In the neckwear patterns, indications are included to knit most sections shorter or longer. These extra instructions will allow you to use the yarn you want while achieving the size that you want.

Knitters are always coming up with new ideas to modify a pattern, and I strongly encourage you to try what you have in mind. I'm sure that with a good understanding of gauge and a little bit of math, you already have or can develop the skills to modify any pattern to your liking. Be confident. The worst that can happen is that you'll need to unravel your work. But no matter the result, you'll have learned something.

A Final Word on Gauge

Handmade isn't machine-made, and our knitting tension varies over the course of a day, a week, a year and even a project. A swatch, even a big one, won't have the same weight as a garment; therefore, the finished garment will probably have a looser gauge. No matter how mindfully you knit and how accurately you do your swatch, keep in mind that gauge is never perfect. And that's okay!

The Terrene Collection

Nature-Inspired Textures for Easy, Everyday Wear

I live in a place where the winters are quite harsh and the midseasons are on the colder side as well. But to tell you the truth, no matter what the weather is like outside, I'm always cold. For us chilly people—and I suspect that a considerable number of knitters are just like me—knitwear is the apogee of garments. Most days of the year, I want to wear either a knitted sweater or a shawl (or both!) over my shoulders. I always welcome cozy socks and as soon as I step outside, I need to wear a knitted hat.

Named for the earthy beauty of the world and the stability of the ground, The *Terrene* Collection consists of four convenient patterns that will provide some extra warmth for your days spent inside and outside the house. These patterns give a great dose of comfort, and they are made of lace patterns that will remind you of the beauty of nature. The Pine Cone Sweater (page 23) has a classic circular yoke and, as its name implies, a pine cone pattern that is just as easy to knit as the finished sweater is easy to wear. The Harvest Moon Shawl (page 33), on the other hand, is a more challenging project with colorwork and bobbles, which promises to never be boring and to add a touch of originality to any outfit.

Pine Cone Sweater

The Pine Cone Sweater is one of those basics that you will wear again and again. It's warm and cozy, with a simple straight silhouette that goes with everything. It is just what you need in your everyday life. Its embellishments are minimal, with a circular yoke that makes this simple, classic design stand out. The pine cone lace pattern on the yoke starts small around the neck and gets larger as it moves around the bust.

Construction

This sweater is worked in the round from the top down, starting with ribbing, which is followed by a circular yoke. Once the yoke is completed, the stitches from the sleeves are placed on hold and the body is worked, ending with more ribbing. The sleeves' stitches are then put back on live needles and the sleeves are worked down to the wrist, ending with ribbing for a stretchy fit.

Skill Level: Intermediate

Sizes

- 1 (2, 3, 4) (5, 6, 7, 8) (9, 10, 11)

Finished Measurements

- **Garment circumference at bust:** 32 (34, 36.75, 38) (40.25, 42.5, 45.25, 47.75) (53.5, 54, 59.75) inches / 81.5 (86.5, 93.5, 96.5) (102, 108, 115, 121.5) (136, 137, 152) cm

- **Recommended ease:** To be worn with approximately 1 to 5 inches (2.5 to 13 cm) of positive ease. Pick a size larger than your bust circumference. Sample shown is knit in size 3, worn with 2.75 inches (7 cm) of ease.

Materials

YARN
DK weight, The Yarn Collective Bloomsbury DK (100% merino wool), 263 yds (240 m) per 100-g skein

YARDAGE/METERAGE
1035 (1104, 1191, 1253) (1336, 1440, 1530, 1640) (1873, 1970, 2229) yds / 946 (1009, 1089, 1146) (1222, 1317, 1399, 1500) (1713, 1801, 2038) m

SHOWN IN
Moss [4 (5, 5, 5) (6, 6, 6, 7) (8, 8, 9) skeins]

NEEDLES
For ribbing: US 4 (3.5 mm), 24- or 32-inch (60- or 80-cm) circular needle

For body and sleeves: US 6 (4 mm), 24- or 32-inch (60- or 80-cm) circular needle

NOTIONS
1 stitch marker

2 stitch holders

Tapestry needle

Gauge

23 sts × 30 rnds = 4 inches (10 cm) in stockinette stitch in the round using larger needle (blocked)

Important note: Take time to check your gauge. This will ensure correct fit and yarn quantity.

[continued]

ABBREVIATIONS	
BO	bind off
BOR	beginning of round
cdd	central double decrease
CO	cast on
dec('d)	decrease(d)
inc'd	increase(d)
k	knit
k2tog	knit two together
k3tog	knit three together
m	marker
m1r	make one right
m1l	make one left
p	purl
pm	place marker
rnd(s)	round(s)
sl	slip
ssk	slip slip knit
sssk	slip slip slip knit
st(s)	stitch(es)
St st	stockinette stitch
yo	yarn over
Dec4to1R	decrease 4 to 1 right leaning = k2tog, sl back to left-hand needle, pass 2 sts over the last st created, sl to right-hand needle
Dec4to1L	decrease 4 to 1 left leaning = sl 2, k2tog, pass 2 sl sts over last st created
Dec5to1R	decrease 5 to 1 right leaning = k3tog, sl back to left-hand needle, pass 2 sts over the last st created, sl to right-hand needle
Dec5to1L	decrease 5 to 1 left leaning = sl 2, k3tog, pass 2 sl sts over last st created

Pine Cone Sweater Pattern

SETUP AND NECKBAND
With smaller needles, CO 102 (108, 114, 120) (126, 132, 114, 124) (134, 144, 154) sts.

Join to work in the round and pm to indicate BOR.

Work in (k1, p1) ribbing for 1 inch (2.5 cm).

Switch to larger needles.

YOKE

SIZES 7–11 ONLY
Setup rnd: K1, m1l, k to end.

[102 (108, 114, 120) (126, 132, 115, 125) (135, 145, 155) sts]

ALL SIZES
Work 61 (61, 61, 69) (69, 69, 78, 78) (78, 90, 90) rnds from Yoke Pattern 1 (1, 1, 2) (2, 2, 3, 3) (3, 4, 4), following the charts (pages 30–32) or written instructions below. Then proceed to **End of Yoke** (page 27). [306 (324, 342, 360) (378, 396, 414, 450) (486, 522, 558) sts]

YOKE PATTERN 1 [SIZES 1 (2, 3)]
Rnd 1: (K5, p1) around.

Rnd 2: (M1r, k5, m1l, p1) around. [34 (36, 38) sts inc'd]

Rnd 3: (K7, p1) around.

Rnd 4: [K2tog, (yo, k1) 3 times, yo, ssk, p1] around. [34 (36, 38) sts inc'd]

Rnds 5–7: (K9, p1) around.

Rnd 8: [K3tog, (yo, k1) 3 times, yo, sssk, p1] around.

Rnd 9: (K9, p1) around.

Rnds 10–13: Repeat rnds 6–9.

Rnd 14: (M1r, k9, m1l, p1) around. [34 (36, 38) sts inc'd]

Rnd 15: (K11, p1) around.

Rnd 16: [K3tog, (yo, k1) 5 times, yo, sssk, p1] around. [34 (36, 38) sts inc'd]

Rnd 17–19: (K13, p1) around.

Rnd 20: [Dec4to1R, (yo, k1) 5 times, yo, Dec4to1L, p1] around.

Rnd 21: (K13, p1) around.

Rnds 22–41: Repeat rnds 18–21.

Rnd 42: (M1r, k13, m1l, p1) around. [34 (36, 38) sts inc'd]

Rnd 43: (K15, p1) around.

Rnd 44: [Dec4to1R, (yo, k1) 7 times, yo, Dec4to1L, p1] around. [34 (36, 38) sts inc'd]

Rnd 45–47: (K17, p1) around.

Rnd 48: [Dec5to1R, (yo, k1) 7 times, yo, Dec5to1L, p1] around.

Rnds 49–52: Repeat rnds 45–48.

Rnd 53: (Yo, ssk, k13, k2tog, yo, k1) around.

Rnd 54: (K1, yo, ssk, k11, k2tog, yo, k2) around.

Rnd 55: (K2, yo, ssk, k9, k2tog, yo, k3) around.

Rnd 56: (K3, yo, ssk, k1, k2tog, yo, k1, yo, ssk, k1, k2tog, yo, k4) around.

Rnd 57: (K4, yo, ssk, k5, k2tog, yo, k5) around.

Rnd 58: (K5, yo, ssk, k3, k2tog, yo, k6) around.

Rnd 59: (K6, yo, ssk, k1, k2tog, yo, k7) around.

Rnd 60: (K7, yo, cdd, yo, k8) around.

Rnd 61: K all sts.

YOKE PATTERN 2 [SIZES 4 (5, 6)]

Rnd 1: (K5, p1) around.

Rnd 2: (M1r, k5, m1l, p1) around. [40 (42, 44) sts inc'd]

Rnd 3: (K7, p1) around.

Rnd 4: [K2tog, (yo, k1) 3 times, yo, ssk, p1] around. [40 (42, 44) sts inc'd]

Rnds 5–7: (K9, p1) around.

Rnd 8: [K3tog, (yo, k1) 3 times, yo, sssk, p1] around.

Rnd 9: (K9, p1) around.

Rnds 10–17: Repeat rnds 6–9.

Rnd 18: (M1r, k9, m1l, p1) around. [40 (42, 44) sts inc'd]

Rnd 19: (K11, p1) around.

Rnd 20: [K3tog, (yo, k1) 5 times, yo, sssk, p1] around. [40 (42, 44) sts inc'd]

Rnds 21–23: (K13, p1) around.

Rnd 24: [Dec4to1R, (yo, k1) 5 times, yo, Dec4to1L, p1] around.

Rnd 25: (K13, p1) around.

Rnds 26–45: Repeat rnds 22–25.

Rnd 46: (M1r, k13, m1l, p1) around. [40 (42, 44) sts inc'd]

Rnd 47: (K15, p1) around.

Rnd 48: [Dec4to1R, (yo, k1) 7 times, yo, Dec4to1L, p1] around. [40 (42, 44) sts inc'd]

Rnds 49–51: (K17, p1) around.

Rnd 52: [Dec5to1R, (yo, k1) 7 times, yo, Dec5to1L, p1] around.

Rnds 53–60: Repeat rnds 49–52.

[continued]

YOKE PATTERN 3 [SIZES 7 (8, 9)]

Rnd 1: (M1r, k4, p1) around. [23 (25, 27) sts inc'd]

Rnd 2: (K5, p1) around.

Rnd 3: (M1r, k5, m1l, p1) around. [46 (50, 54) sts inc'd]

Rnd 4: (K7, p1) around.

Rnd 5: [K2tog, (yo, k1) 3 times, yo, ssk, p1] around. [46 (50, 54) sts inc'd]

Rnds 6–8: (K9, p1) around.

Rnd 9: [K3tog, (yo, k1) 3 times, yo, sssk, p1] around.

Rnds 10–21: Repeat rnds 6–9.

Rnd 22: (K9, p1) around.

Rnd 23: (M1r, k9, m1l, p1) around. [46 (50, 54) sts inc'd]

Rnd 24: (K11, p1) around.

Rnd 25: [K3tog, (yo, k1) 5 times, yo, sssk, p1] around. [46 (50, 54) sts inc'd]

Rnds 26–28: (K13, p1) around.

Rnd 29: [Dec4to1R, (yo, k1) 5 times, yo, Dec4to1L, p1] around.

Rnds 30–53: Repeat rnds 26–29.

Rnd 54: (K13, p1) around.

Rnd 55: (M1r, k13, m1l, p1) around. [46 (50, 54) sts inc'd]

Rnd 56: (K15, p1) around.

Rnd 57: [Dec4to1R, (yo, k1) 7 times, yo, Dec4to1L, p1] around. [46 (50, 54) sts inc'd]

Rnds 58–60: (K17, p1) around.

Rnd 61: [Dec5to1R, (yo, k1) 7 times, yo, Dec5to1L, p1] around.

Rnds 62–69: Repeat rnds 58–61.

Rnd 70: (Yo, ssk, k13, k2tog, yo, k1) around.

Rnd 71: (K1, yo, ssk, k11, k2tog, yo, k2) around.

Rnd 72: (K2, yo, ssk, k9, k2tog, yo, k3) around.

Rnd 73: (K3, yo, ssk, k1, k2tog, yo, k1, yo, ssk, k1, k2tog, yo, k4) around.

Rnd 61: (Yo, ssk, k13, k2tog, yo, k1) around.

Rnd 62: (K1, yo, ssk, k11, k2tog, yo, k2) around.

Rnd 63: (K2, yo, ssk, k9, k2tog, yo, k3) around.

Rnd 64: (K3, yo, ssk, k1, k2tog, yo, k1, yo, ssk, k1, k2tog, yo, k4) around.

Rnd 65: (K4, yo, ssk, k5, k2tog, yo, k5) around.

Rnd 66: (K5, yo, ssk, k3, k2tog, yo, k6) around.

Rnd 67: (K6, yo, ssk, k1, k2tog, yo, k7) around.

Rnd 68: (K7, yo, cdd, yo, k8) around.

Rnd 69: K all sts.

Rnd 74: (K4, yo, ssk, k5, k2tog, yo, k5) around.

Rnd 75: (K5, yo, ssk, k3, k2tog, yo, k6) around.

Rnd 76: (K6, yo, ssk, k1, k2tog, yo, k7) around.

Rnd 77: (K7, yo, cdd, yo, k8) around.

Rnd 78: K all sts.

YOKE PATTERN 4 [SIZES 10 (11)]

Rnd 1: (M1r, k4, p1) around. [29 (31) sts inc'd]

Rnd 2: (K5, p1) around.

Rnd 3: (M1r, k5, m1l, p1) around. [58 (62) sts inc'd]

Rnd 4: (K7, p1) around.

Rnd 5: [K2tog, (yo, k1) 3 times, yo, ssk, p1] around. [58 (62) sts inc'd]

Rnds 6–8: (K9, p1) around.

Rnd 9: [K3tog, (yo, k1) 3 times, yo, sssk, p1] around.

Rnds 10–25: Repeat rnds 6–9.

Rnd 26: (K9, p1) around.

Rnd 27: (M1r, k9, m1l, p1) around. [58 (62) sts inc'd]

Rnd 28: (K11, p1) around.

Rnd 29: [K3tog, (yo, k1) 5 times, yo, sssk, p1] around. [58 (62) sts inc'd]

Rnds 30–32: (K13, p1) around.

Rnd 33: [Dec4to1R, (yo, k1) 5 times, yo, Dec4to1L, p1] around.

Rnds 34–61: Repeat rnds 30–33.

Rnd 62: (K13, p1) around.

Rnd 63: (M1r, k13, m1l, p1) around. [58 (62) sts inc'd]

Rnd 64: (K15, p1) around.

Rnd 65: [Dec4to1R, (yo, k1) 7 times, yo, Dec4to1L, p1] around. [58 (62) sts inc'd]

Rnds 66–68: (K17, p1) around.

Rnd 69: [Dec5to1R, (yo, k1) 7 times, yo, Dec5to1L, p1] around.

Rnds 70–81: Repeat rnds 66–69.

Rnd 82: (Yo, ssk, k13, k2tog, yo, k1) around.

Rnd 83: (K1, yo, ssk, k11, k2tog, yo, k2) around.

Rnd 84: (K2, yo, ssk, k9, k2tog, yo, k3) around.

Rnd 85: (K3, yo, ssk, k1, k2tog, yo, k1, yo, ssk, k1, k2tog, yo, k4) around.

Rnd 86: (K4, yo, ssk, k5, k2tog, yo, k5) around.

Rnd 87: (K5, yo, ssk, k3, k2tog, yo, k6) around.

Rnd 88: (K6, yo, ssk, k1, k2tog, yo, k7) around.

Rnd 89: (K7, yo, cdd, yo, k8) around.

Rnd 90: K all sts.

END OF YOKE

K all sts for 0 (2, 2, 0) (0, 3, 0, 1) (3, 0, 3) more rnds.

SEPARATE BODY AND SLEEVES

Front: K 88 (94, 102, 105) (112, 118, 126, 133) (148, 151, 168) sts;

Sleeve: Sl 65 (68, 69, 75) (77, 80, 81, 92) (95, 110, 111) sts to holder;

Back: CO 4 (4, 4, 4) (4, 4, 4, 4) (6, 4, 4) sts; k 88 (94, 102, 105) (112, 118, 126, 133) (148, 151, 168) sts; CO 4 (4, 4, 4) (4, 4, 4, 4) (6, 4, 4) sts;

Sleeve: Sl 65 (68, 69, 75) (77, 80, 81, 92) (95, 110, 111) sts to holder.

[**Live st count at bust:** 184 (196, 212, 218) (232, 244, 260, 274) (308, 310, 344) sts]

Pm to indicate BOR and join to work in the rnd.

BODY

K all sts until sweater measures 13.5 (13.5, 14, 14) (14.5, 14.5, 15, 15) (15.5, 15.5, 16) inches / 34.5 (34.5, 35.5, 35.5) (37, 37, 38, 38) (39.5, 39.5, 40.5) cm from underarm or 2.5 inches (6.5 cm) less than the desired finished length.

Work in (k1, p1) ribbing for 2.5 inches (6.5 cm).

BO all sts in pattern.

[continued]

SLEEVES (BOTH WORKED ALIKE)

Join yarn at right side of underarm.

Pick up and k 6 (6, 6, 6) (6, 6, 6, 6) (8, 6, 6) sts from underarm; k 65 (68, 69, 75) (77, 80, 81, 92) (95, 110, 111) sts from holder.

[71 (74, 75, 81) (83, 86, 87, 98) (103, 116, 117) sts]

Join to work in the round, k 3 (3, 3, 3) (3, 3, 3, 3) (4, 3, 3) sts, and pm to indicate BOR.

Work even in St st for 9 (7, 8, 6) (6, 6, 7, 4) (5, 3, 4) rnds.

Continuing in St st, work dec rnds as follows:

Dec rnd: K1, k2tog, k to 3 before m, ssk, k1.

Repeat dec rnd every 9 (7, 8, 6) (6, 6, 7, 4) (5, 3, 4) rnds, 8 (10, 9, 11) (12, 13, 11, 17) (17, 23, 21) times more.

[53 (52, 55, 57) (57, 58, 63, 62) (67, 68, 73) sts]

Work even until sleeve measures 15 (15, 15.25, 15.25) (15.5, 15.5, 15.75, 16) (16.25, 16.25, 16.5) inches / 38 (38, 38.5, 38.5) (39.5, 39.5, 40, 40.5) (41.5, 41.5, 42) cm from joining rnd or 2.5 inches (6.5 cm) less than the desired finished length.

NEXT ROW

Size 1: (K4, ssk) to last 5 sts, k3, ssk. [9 sts dec'd]

Size 2: (K4, ssk) to last 4 sts, k4. [8 sts dec'd]

Size 3: (K4, ssk) to last 7 sts, k5, ssk. [9 sts dec'd]

Sizes 4 and 5: (K5, ssk) to last 8 sts, (k2, ssk) twice. [9 (9) sts dec'd]

Size 6: (K5, ssk) to last 2 sts, k2. [8 sts dec'd]

Size 7: (K5, ssk) around. [9 sts dec'd]

Size 8: (K5, ssk) to last 6 sts, k6. [8 sts dec'd]

Size 9: (K6, ssk) to last 3 sts, k1, ssk. [9 sts dec'd]

Size 10: (K6, ssk) to last 4 sts, k4. [8 sts dec'd]

Size 11: (K7, ssk) to last 10 sts, (k3, ssk) twice. [9 sts dec'd]

[44 (44, 46, 48) (48, 50, 54, 54) (58, 60, 64) sts]

Switch to smaller needles.

Work in (k1, p1) ribbing for 2.5 inches (6.5 cm).

BO all sts in pattern.

FINISHING

Weave in all ends. Block to desired dimensions.

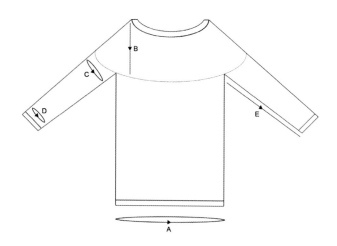

CHART KEY

□	knit
•	purl
O	yo
⼨	m1r
⼩	m1l
∕	k2tog
＼	ssk
⼨	k3tog
⅄	sssk
⋌	sl2, k2tog, p2sso
⼨	k4tog
⋋	sl2, k3tog, p2sso
∕	k5tog
⋀	cdd
▨	no stitch

A: CIRCUMFERENCE AT BUST, WAIST AND HIPS

32 (34, 36.75, 38) (40.25, 42.5, 45.25, 47.75) (53.5, 54, 59.75) inches

81.5 (86.5, 93.5, 96.5) (102, 108, 115, 121.5) (136, 137, 152) cm

B: YOKE LENGTH

8.25 (8.5, 8.5, 9.25) (9.25, 9.5, 10.5, 10.5) (10.75, 12, 12.5) inches

21 (21.5, 21.5, 23.5) (23.5, 24, 26.5, 26.5) (27.5, 30.5, 32) cm

C: SLEEVE CIRCUMFERENCE AT TOP ARM

12.25 (12.75, 13, 14) (14.5, 15, 15.25, 17) (18, 20.25, 20.25) inches

31 (32.5, 33, 35.5) (37, 38, 38.5, 43) (45.5, 51.5, 51.5) cm

D: SLEEVE CIRCUMFERENCE AT WRIST

7.75 (7.75, 8, 8.25) (8.25, 8.75, 9.5, 9.5) (10, 10.5, 11.25) inches

19.5 (19.5, 20.5, 21) (21, 22, 24, 24) (25.5, 26.5, 28.5) cm

E: SLEEVE LENGTH AT UNDERARM

17.5 (17.5, 17.75, 17.75) (18, 18, 18.25, 18.5) (18.75, 18.75, 19) inches

44.5 (44.5, 45, 45) (45.5, 45.5, 46.5, 47) (47.5, 47.5, 48.5) cm

[continued]

YOKE PATTERN 1

YOKE PATTERN 2

YOKE PATTERN 3
(BOTTOM)

YOKE PATTERN 3 (TOP)

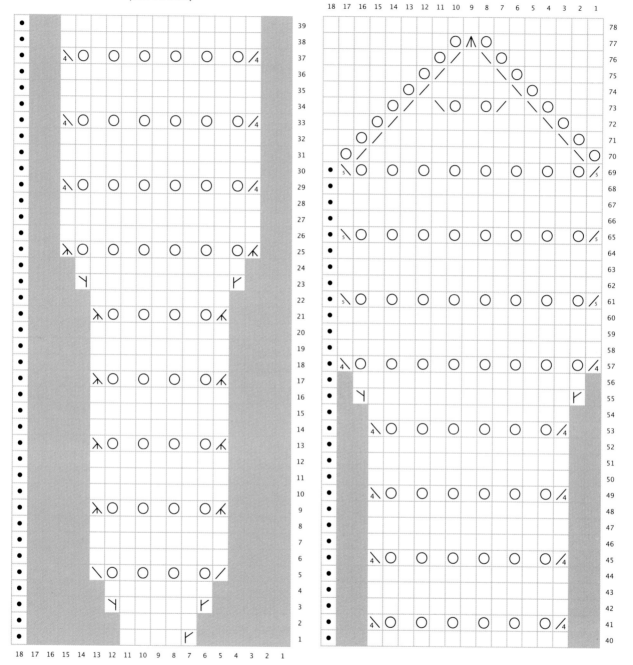

YOKE PATTERN 4 (BOTTOM)

YOKE PATTERN 4 (TOP)

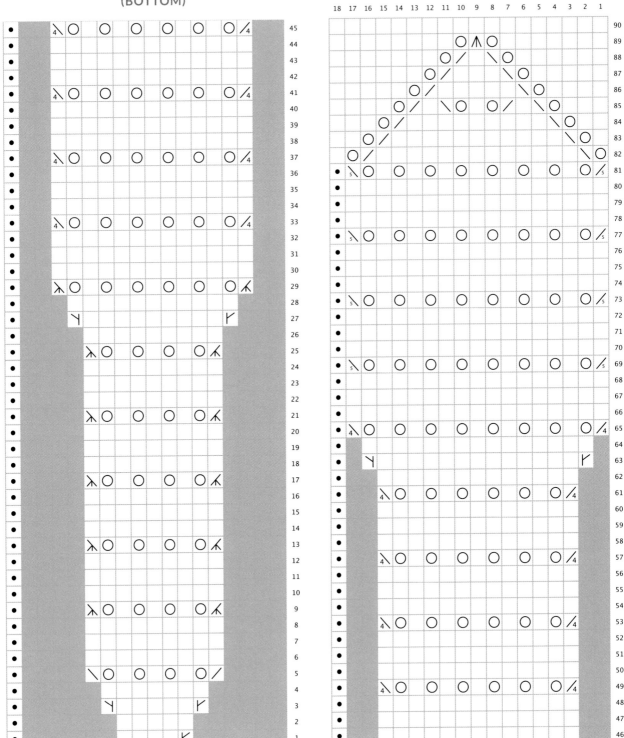

Harvest Moon Shawl

Near the beginning of autumn, the crops are at their fullest and are ready for the final harvest of the season, just before it gets too cold for us to go out and for plants to grow. At this time of year, there is a phenomenon called the harvest moon. This full moon rises earlier and is brighter than usual. Historically, it helped famers harvest the crops until late at night. The Harvest Moon Shawl is an allegory of the abundance of crops at this time of year. It is covered in bobbles that are worked in a contrasting color to completely stand out from the background. Paired with lace patterns and a bit of stranded colorwork, this pattern will whet your appetite for a fun knitting challenge.

Construction

This shawl is worked from the top down, starting with a garter tab from which stitches are picked up to work in a triangular shape. The edges of the shawl are made in garter stitch, while the body combines stranded colorwork with a lace pattern enhanced with bobbles. The bottom of the shawl gradually shifts from the lace and colorwork pattern to finish with a ribbing made with the main color. This shawl is adaptable in size—you can knit the body section longer or shorter to create the perfect shawl for you, though your yardage will vary.

Skill Level: Advanced

Size

- One size for adults

Finished Measurements

- 44.5 inches (113 cm) wide at top edge
- 20 inches (51 cm) long at point, blocked

Materials

YARN
Sport weight, Magpie Nest Sport (100% non-superwash Corriedale wool), 350 yds (320 m) per 100-g skein

YARDAGE / METERAGE
MC: 350 yds (320 m)
CC: 310 yds (283 m)

SHOWN IN
MC: Castaway (1 skein)
CC: Twilight Honey (1 skein)

Any fingering to DK weight yarn can be used for this pattern. Gauge, yardage and final size will vary.

NEEDLES
US 3 (3.25 mm), 32-inch (80-cm) circular needle, or size needed to obtain gauge

Important note: Gauge can vary according to your yarn and needle size. If your gauge differs, your shawl will have different dimensions from the prototype. Make sure to plan for more yardage if you use a different yarn or wish to achieve a larger size.

NOTIONS
4 stitch markers
Tapestry needle
Crochet hook to make bobbles

(continued)

Gauge

24 sts × 36 rows = 4 inches (10 cm) in Body pattern (blocked)

Important note: Take time to check your gauge. This will ensure correct fit and yarn quantity.

Special Techniques

Bobbles (page 152): For this pattern, I recommend doing 4 repetitions of (k1, yo) in the same stitch.

ABBREVIATIONS	
BO	bind off
CC	contrast color
CO	cast on
inc'd	increased
k	knit
k2tog	knit two together
m	marker
m1l	make one left
m1r	make one right
mb	make bobble
MC	main color
p	purl
p2tog	purl two together
pm	place marker
rem	remaining
RS	right side
sm	slip marker
ssk	slip slip knit
ssp	slip slip purl
st(s)	stitch(es)
WS	wrong side
yo	yarn over

Harvest Moon Shawl Pattern

You may work this shawl either from the charts (pages 42–43) or from the written instructions. Look for the separate sections as you proceed through the pattern.

SETUP

With CC, CO 3 sts.

K all sts for 14 rows.

Next row (RS): K3, do not turn, pick up and k 9 sts along the edge, pick up and k 3 sts from CO sts. [15 sts]

Next row (WS): K3, pm, p3, pm, p3 (middle sts), pm, p3, pm, k3.

PLAIN ROWS

Plain RS row: K3, sm, m1l, k to next m, m1r, sm, k3, sm, m1l, k to next m, m1r, sm, k3. [4 sts inc'd.]

Plain WS row: K3, sm, p to last 3 sts, sm, k3.

Work plain rows, 3 times total (6 rows). [27 sts (3 border sts, 9 wing sts, 3 middle sts, 9 wing sts, 3 border sts)]

TOP SECTION

Using CC on rows 1–56, MC and CC on rows 57–62 and MC on rows 63–64, work 64 rows of the Top Section pattern. Work either the written instructions or the chart instructions that follow. Then proceed to **Body Section** (page 38).

TOP SECTION WRITTEN INSTRUCTIONS

WITH CC:
Row 1 (RS): (K3, m1l, k4, mb, k4, m1r) twice, k3. [31 sts]

Row 2 (WS): K3, p25, k3.

Row 3: (K3, m1l, yo, ssk, k2, mb, k1, mb, k2, k2tog, yo, m1r) twice, k3. [35 sts]

Row 4: K3, p2, yo, p2tog, p5, ssp, yo, p7, yo, p2tog, p5, ssp, yo, p2, k3.

[continued]

Row 5: (K3, m1l, k13, m1r) twice, k3. [39 sts]

Row 6: K3, p1, yo, p2, p2tog, p5, ssp, p2, yo, p5, yo, p2, p2tog, p5, ssp, p2, yo, p1, k3.

Row 7: (K3, m1l, k2, yo, k2, ssk, k3, k2tog, k2, yo, k2, m1r) twice, k3. [43 sts]

Row 8: K3, p4, yo, p2, p2tog, p1, ssp, p2, yo, p11, yo, p2, p2tog, p1, ssp, p2, yo, p4, k3.

Row 9: (K3, m1l, mb, k5, k2tog, yo, k1, yo, ssk, k5, mb, m1r) twice, k3. [47 sts]

Row 10: K3, p6, ssp, yo, p3, yo, p2tog, p15, ssp, yo, p3, yo, p2tog, p6, k3.

Row 11: (K3, m1l, mb, k1, mb, k2, k2tog, yo, k5, yo, ssk, k2, mb, k1, mb, m1r) twice, k3. [51 sts]

Row 12: K3, p5, ssp, yo, p7, yo, p2tog, p13, ssp, yo, p7, yo, p2tog, p5, k3.

Row 13: (K3, m1l, k6, k2tog, k2, yo, k1, yo, k2, ssk, k6, m1r) twice, k3. [55 sts]

Row 14: K3, p6, ssp, p2, yo, p3, yo, p2, p2tog, p15, ssp, p2, yo, p3, yo, p2, p2tog, p6, k3.

Row 15: (K3, m1l, k5, k2tog, k2, yo, k5, yo, k2, ssk, k5, m1r) twice, k3. [59 sts]

Row 16: K3, p5, ssp, p2, yo, p7, yo, p2, p2tog, p13, ssp, p2, yo, p7, yo, p2, p2tog, p5, k3.

Row 17: (K3, m1l, k2, k2tog, yo, k1, yo, ssk, k5, mb, k5, k2tog, yo, k1, yo, ssk, k2, m1r) twice, k3. [63 sts]

Row 18: K3, p2, ssp, yo, p3, yo, p2tog, p9, ssp, yo, p3, yo, p2tog, p7, ssp, yo, p3, yo, p2tog, p9, ssp, yo, p3, yo, p2tog, p2, k3.

Row 19: (K3, m1l, k1, k2tog, yo, k5, yo, ssk, k2, mb, k1, mb, k2, k2tog, yo, k5, yo, ssk, k1, m1r) twice, k3. [67 sts]

Row 20: K3, p1, (ssp, yo, p7, yo, p2tog, p5) three times, ssp, yo, p7, yo, p2tog, p1, k3.

Row 21: (K3, m1l, k2, k2tog, k2, yo, k1, yo, k2, ssk, k7, k2tog, k2, yo, k1, yo, k2, ssk, k2, m1r) twice, k3. [71 sts]

Row 22: K3, p2, ssp, p2, yo, p3, yo, p2, p2tog, p5, ssp, p2, yo, p3, yo, p2, p2tog, p7, ssp, p2, yo, p3, yo, p2, p2tog, p5, ssp, p2, yo, p3, yo, p2, p2tog, p2, k3.

Row 23: (K3, m1l, k1, k2tog, k2, yo, k5, yo, k2, ssk, k3, k2tog, k2, yo, k5, yo, k2, ssk, k1, m1r) twice, k3. [75 sts]

Row 24: K3, (p1, ssp, p2, yo, p7, yo, p2, p2tog) twice, p5, (ssp, p2, yo, p7, yo, p2, p2tog, p1) twice, k3.

Row 25: [K3, m1l, (k1, yo, ssk, k5, mb, k5, k2tog, yo) twice, k1, m1r] twice, k3. [79 sts]

Row 26: K3, (p3, yo, p2tog, p9, ssp, yo) twice, p9, (yo, p2tog, p9, ssp, yo, p3) twice, k3.

Row 27: (K3, m1l, k4, yo, ssk, k2, mb, k1, mb, k2, k2tog, yo, k5, yo, ssk, k2, mb, k1, mb, k2, k2tog, yo, k4, m1r) twice, k3. [83 sts]

Row 28: K3, p6, yo, p2tog, p5, ssp, yo, p7, yo, p2tog, p5, ssp, yo, p15, yo, p2tog, p5, ssp, yo, p7, yo, p2tog, p5, ssp, yo, p6, k3.

Row 29: (K3, m1l, k3, yo, k2, ssk, k7, k2tog, k2, yo, k1, yo, k2, ssk, k7, k2tog, k2, yo, k3, m1r) twice, k3. [87 sts]

Row 30: K3, p5, yo, p2, p2tog, p5, ssp, p2, yo, p3, yo, p2, p2tog, p5, ssp, p2, yo, p13, yo, p2, p2tog, p5, ssp, p2, yo, p3, yo, p2, p2tog, p5, ssp, p2, yo, p5, k3.

Row 31: (K3, m1l, k6, yo, k2, ssk, k3, k2tog, k2, yo, k5, yo, k2, ssk, k3, k2tog, k2, yo, k6, m1r) twice, k3. [91 sts]

Row 32: K3, p8, yo, p2, p2tog, p1, ssp, p2, yo, p7, yo, p2, p2tog, p1, ssp, p2, yo, p19, yo, p2, p2tog, p1, ssp, p2, yo, p7, yo, p2, p2tog, p1, ssp, p2, yo, p8, k3.

Row 33: [K3, m1l, k4, (mb, k5, k2tog, yo, k1, yo, ssk, k5) twice, mb, k4, m1r] twice, k3. [95 sts]

Row 34: K3, p10, ssp, yo, p3, yo, p2tog, p9, ssp, yo, p3, yo, p2tog, p23, ssp, yo, p3, yo, p2tog, p9, ssp, yo, p3, yo, p2tog, p10, k3.

Row 35: [K3, m1l, (yo, ssk, k2, mb, k1, mb, k2, k2tog, yo, k5) twice, yo, ssk, k2, mb, k1, mb, k2, k2tog, yo, m1r] twice, k3. [99 sts]

Row 36: K3, p2, (yo, p2tog, p5, ssp, yo, p7) 5 times, yo, p2tog, p5, ssp, yo, p2, k3.

Row 37: (K3, m1l, k10, k2tog, k2, yo, k1, yo, k2, ssk, k7, k2tog, k2, yo, k1, yo, k2, ssk, k10, m1r) twice, k3. [103 sts]

Row 38: K3, p1, (yo, p2, p2tog, p5, ssp, p2, yo, p3) twice, yo, p2, p2tog, p5, ssp, p2, yo, p5, (yo, p2, p2tog, p5, ssp, p2, yo, p3) twice, yo, p2, p2tog, p5, ssp, p2, yo, p1, k3.

Row 39: [K3, m1l, k2, (yo, k2, ssk, k3, k2tog, k2, yo, k5) twice, yo, k2, ssk, k3, k2tog, k2, yo, k2, m1r] twice, k3. [107 sts]

Row 40: K3, p4, (yo, p2, p2tog, p1, ssp, p2, yo, p7) twice, yo, p2, p2tog, p1, ssp, p2, yo, p11, (yo, p2, p2tog, p1, ssp, p2, yo, p7) twice, yo, p2, p2tog, p1, ssp, p2, yo, p4, k3.

Row 41: (K3, m1l, *mb, k5, k2tog, yo, k1, yo, ssk, k5; repeat from * twice more, mb, m1r) twice, k3. [111 sts]

Row 42: K3, (p2, *p4, ssp, yo, p3, yo, p2tog, p5; repeat from * twice more, p4) twice; on the last repeat, end p1, k3 instead of p4.

Row 43: (K3, m1l, mb, *k1, mb, k2, k2tog, yo, k5, yo, ssk, k2, mb; repeat from * twice more, k1, mb, m1r) twice, k3. [115 sts]

Row 44: K3, (p3, *p2, ssp, yo, p7, yo, p2tog, p3; repeat from * twice more, p5) twice; on the last repeat, end p2, k3 instead of p5.

Row 45: (K3, m1l, k2, *k4, k2tog, k2, yo, k1, yo, k2, ssk, k3; repeat from * twice more, k3, m1r) twice, k3. [119 sts]

Row 46: K3, (p4, *p2, ssp, p2, yo, p3, yo, p2, p2tog, p3; repeat from * twice more, p6) twice; on the last repeat, end p3, k3 instead of p6.

Row 47: (K3, m1l, k3, *k2, k2tog, k2, yo, k5, yo, k2, ssk, k1; repeat from * twice more, k4, m1r) twice, k3. [123 sts]

Row 48: K3, (p5, *ssp, p2, yo, p7, yo, p2, p2tog, p1; repeat from * twice more, p7) twice; on the last repeat, end p4, k3 instead of p7.

Row 49: (K3, m1l, k2, k2tog, yo, *k1, yo, ssk, k5, mb, k5, k2tog, yo; repeat from * twice more, k1, yo, ssk, k2, m1r) twice, k3. [127 sts]

Row 50: K3, (p2, ssp, yo, p2 *p1, yo, p2tog, p9, ssp, yo, p2; repeat from * twice more, p1, yo, p2tog, p5) twice; on the last repeat, end p2, k3 instead of p5.

Row 51: (K3, m1l, k1, k2tog, yo, k2, *k3, yo, ssk, k2, mb, k1, mb, k2, k2tog, yo, k2; repeat from * twice more, k3, yo, ssk, k1, m1r) twice, k3. [131 sts]

Row 52: K3, (p1, ssp, yo, p4, *p3, yo, p2tog, p5, ssp, yo, p4; repeat from * twice more, p3, yo, p2tog, p4) twice; on the last repeat, end p1, k3 instead of p4.

Row 53: (K3, m1l, k2, k2tog, k2, yo, *k1, yo, k2, ssk, k7, k2tog, k2, yo; repeat from * twice more, k1, yo, k2, ssk, k2, m1r) twice, k3. [135 sts]

Row 54: K3, (p2, ssp, p2, yo, p2, *p1, yo, p2, p2tog, p5, ssp, p2, yo, p2; repeat from * twice more, p1, yo, p2, p2tog, p5) twice; on the last repeat, end p2, k3 instead of p5.

Row 55: (K3, m1l, k1, k2tog, k2, yo, k2, *k3, yo, k2, ssk, k3, k2tog, k2, yo, k2; repeat from * twice more, k3, yo, k2, ssk, k1, m1r) twice, k3. [139 sts]

Row 56: K3, (p1, ssp, p2, yo, p4 *p3, yo, p2, p2tog, p1, ssp, p2, yo, p4; repeat from * twice more, p3, yo, p2, p2tog, p4) twice; on the last repeat, end p1, k3 instead of p4.

[continued]

WITH MC AND CC:

Row 57: (K3 MC, m1l MC, k2 MC, k6 CC, *mb CC, k6 CC, k1 MC, mb CC, k1 MC, k6 CC; repeat from * twice more, mb CC, k CC, k2 MC, m1r MC) twice, k3 MC. [143 sts]

Row 58: K3 MC, (p4 MC, p6 CC, *p5 CC, p5 MC, p6 CC; repeat from * twice more, p5 CC, p7 MC) twice; on the last repeat, end p4, k3 instead of p7.

Row 59: (K3 MC, m1l MC, k5 MC, k3 CC, mb CC, *k1 CC, mb CC, k3 CC, k7 MC, k3 CC, mb CC; repeat from * twice more, k1 CC, mb CC, k3 CC, k5 MC, m1r MC) twice, k3 MC. [147 sts]

Row 60: K3 MC, (p7 MC, p4 CC, *p3 CC, p9 MC, p4 CC; repeat from * twice more, p3 CC, p10 MC) twice; on the last repeat, end p7, k3 instead of p10.

Row 61: (K3 MC, m1l MC, k8 MC, k2 CC, *k3 CC, k11 MC, k2 CC; repeat from * twice more, k3 CC, k8 MC, m1r MC) twice, k3 MC. [151 sts]

Row 62: K3 MC, (p10 MC, p2 CC, *p1 CC, p13 MC, p2 CC; repeat from * twice more, p1 CC, p13 MC) twice; on the last repeat, end p10, k3 instead of p13.

Cut CC.

WITH MC:

Row 63: (K3, sm, m1l, k to m, m1r, sm) twice, k3. [155 sts]

Row 64: K3, p to last marker, k3.

Stitch count: 155 sts (3 border sts, 73 wing sts, 3 middle sts, 73 wing sts, 3 border sts)

TOP SECTION CHART INSTRUCTIONS

The Top Chart (page 42) is worked twice on each row: once after the first garter edge to the middle stitches, and once more after the middle stitches to the last garter edge. Work the same row of the chart on both sides of the shawl.

The garter edges and middle stitches are worked with CC on rows 1–56, MC and CC on rows 57–62 and with MC on rows 63–64.

Cut CC after row 62.

Starting at row 1 of Top Chart and working your way to the end of the chart, work all 64 rows the following way:

RS row: K3, sm, work from Top Chart to next m, sm, k3, sm, work same row of chart to next m, sm, k3. [4 sts inc'd]

WS row: K3, sm, work from Top Chart to next m, sm, p3, sm, work same row of chart to next m, sm, k3.

Stitch count: 155 sts (3 border sts, 73 wing sts, 3 middle sts, 73 wing sts, 3 border sts)

BODY SECTION

Note that bobbles are made using CC. On rows 1 and 9, carry CC while knitting, using the stranded colorwork technique. Cut CC at the end of the row.

Using MC for the whole pattern and CC to work bobbles, work the whole pattern 4 times (64 rows). Note that you can work the pattern fully as many times as desired (stitch count and yardage required will vary). Work either the written instructions or the chart instructions that follow. Then proceed to **Border Section** (page 39).

BODY SECTION WRITTEN INSTRUCTIONS

- -

Note: Stitch count indicates total stitches after each repetition and looks like this: [1st repetition / 2nd repetition / 3rd repetition / 4th repetition].

- -

Join CC to work bobbles.

Row 1 (RS): (K3, m1l, k4, *mb, k7; repeat from * to 5 sts before m, mb, k4, m1r) twice, k3. [159 sts / 191 sts / 223 sts / 255 sts]

Cut CC.

Row 2 and all WS rows: K3, p to last m, k3.

Row 3: (K3, m1l, k to next m, m1r) twice, k3. [163 sts / 195 sts / 227 sts / 259 sts]

Row 5: Repeat row 3. [167 sts / 199 sts / 231 sts / 263 sts]

Row 7: Repeat row 3. [171 sts / 203 sts / 235 sts / 267 sts]

Join CC to work bobbles.

Row 9: (K3, m1l, *mb, k7; repeat from * to 1 st before m, mb, m1r) twice, k3. [175 sts / 207 sts / 239 sts / 271 sts]

Cut CC.

Row 11: Repeat row 3. [179 sts / 211 sts / 243 sts / 275 sts]

Row 13: Repeat row 3. [183 sts / 215 sts / 247 sts / 279 sts]

Row 15: Repeat row 3. [187 sts / 219 sts / 251 sts / 283 sts]

Row 16: Repeat row 2.

Stitch count: 283 sts (3 border sts, 137 wing sts, 3 middle sts, 137 wing sts, 3 border sts)

BODY SECTION CHART INSTRUCTIONS

The Body Chart (page 43) is worked twice on each row: once after the first garter edge to the middle stitches, and once more after the middle stitches to the last garter edge. Work the same row of chart on both sides of the shawl.

Garter edge and middle stitches are worked with MC.

Join CC at rows 1 and 9 and cut CC after completing each of these rows.

Starting at row 1 of Body Chart and working your way to the end of the chart, work the chart fully 4 times (64 rows total), the following way:

RS row: K3, sm, work from Body Chart to next m, sm, k3, sm, work same row of chart to next m, sm, k3. [4 sts inc'd]

WS row: K3, sm, work from Body Chart to next m, sm, p3, sm, work same row of chart to next m, sm, k3.

Stitch count: 283 sts (3 border sts, 137 wing sts, 3 middle sts, 137 wing sts, 3 border sts)

BORDER SECTION

Using CC and MC on rows 1, 4–9, 17–22, MC on rows 2–3, 23–28 and CC on rows 10–16, work 28 rows of the Border Section pattern. Work either the written instructions or the chart instructions that follow. Then proceed to **Finishing** (page 41).

BORDER SECTION WRITTEN INSTRUCTIONS

WITH MC AND CC:
Row 1 (RS): (K3 MC, m1l MC, k4 MC, *mb CC, k7 MC; repeat from * to 5 sts before m, mb, k4, m1r) twice, k3. [287 sts]

Cut CC.

WITH MC:
Row 2 (WS): K3, p to last m, k3.

Row 3: (K3, m1l, k to next m, m1r) twice, k3. [291 sts]

WITH MC AND CC:
Row 4: K3 MC, (p5 MC, p3 CC, p7 MC, *p6 MC, p3 CC, p7 MC; repeat from * to 14 sts before m, p6 MC, p3 CC, p8 MC) twice; on the last repeat, end p5, k3 instead of p8.

[continued]

Row 5: (K3 MC, m1l MC, k4 MC, k5 CC, k5 MC, *k6 MC, k5 CC, k5 MC; repeat from * to 15 sts before m, k6 MC, k5 CC, k4 MC, m1r MC) twice, k3 MC. [295 sts]

Row 6: K3 MC, (p4 MC, p7 CC, p5 MC, *p4 MC, p7 CC, p5 MC; repeat from * to 15 sts before m, 4 MC, p7 CC, p7 MC) twice; on the last repeat, end p4, k3 instead of p7.

Row 7: (K3 MC, m1l MC, k3 MC, k9 CC, k3 MC, *k4 MC, k9 CC, k3 MC; repeat from * to 16 sts before m, k4 MC, k9 CC, k3 MC, m1r MC) twice, k3 MC. [299 sts]

Row 8: K3 MC, (p3 MC, p11 CC, p3 MC, *p2 MC, p11 CC, p3 MC; repeat from * to next m, p3 MC) twice; on the last repeat, end k3 instead of p3.

Row 9: (K3 CC, m1l CC, *mb CC, k1 MC, k13 CC, k1 MC; repeat from * to 1 st before m, mb CC, m1r CC) twice, k3 CC. [303 sts]

Cut MC.

WITH CC:

Row 10: K3, (p2, *p4, ssp, yo, p3, yo, p2tog, p5; repeat from * to 1 st before m, p4) twice; on the last repeat, end p1, k3.

Row 11: (K3, m1l, mb, *k1, mb, k2, k2tog, yo, k5, yo, ssk, k2, mb; repeat from * to 2 sts before m, k1, mb, m1r) twice, k3. [307 sts]

Row 12: K3, (p3, *p2, ssp, yo, p7, yo, p2tog, p3; repeat from * to 2 sts before m, p5) twice; on the last repeat, end p2, k5 instead of p3.

Row 13: (K3, m1l, k2, *mb, k7; repeat from * to 3 sts before m, mb, k2, m1r) twice, k3. [311 sts]

Row 14: K3 (p4, *p3, yo, p2tog, p5, ssp, yo, p4; repeat from * to 3 sts before m, p6) twice; on the last repeat, end p3, k3 instead of p6.

Row 15: (K3, m1l, k2, mb, *k1, mb, k3, yo, ssk, k3, k2tog, yo, k3, mb; repeat from * to 4 sts before m, k1, mb, k2, m1r) twice, k3. [315 sts]

Row 16: K3, (p5, *p5, yo, p2tog, p1, ssp, yo, p6; repeat from * to 4 sts before marker, p7) twice; on the last repeat, end p4, k3 instead of p7.

WITH MC AND CC:

Row 17: (K3 CC, m1l CC, k3 CC, k1 MC, *mb CC, k1 MC, k13 CC, k1 MC; repeat from * to 5 sts before m, mb CC, k1 MC, k3 CC, m1r CC) twice, k3 CC. [319 sts]

Row 18: K3 CC, (p3 CC, p1 MC, k1 MC, p1 MC, *k1 MC, p1 MC, p11 CC, p1 MC, k1 MC, p1 MC; repeat from * to 5 sts before m, k1 MC, p1 MC, p6 CC) twice; on the last repeat, end p3 CC, k3 CC.

Row 19: (K3 CC, m1l CC, k2 CC, k2 MC, p1 MC, *k1 MC, p1 MC, k2 MC, k9 CC, k2 MC, p1 MC; repeat from * to 6 sts before m, k1 MC, p1 MC, k2 MC, k2 CC, m1r CC) twice, k3 CC. [323 sts]

Row 20: K3 CC, [p2 CC, (p1 MC, k1 MC) twice, p1 MC, *(k1 MC, p1 MC) twice, p7 CC, (p1 MC, k1 MC) twice, p1 MC; repeat from * to 6 sts before m, (k1 MC, p1 MC) twice, p5 CC] twice; on the last repeat, end p2 CC, k3 CC.

Row 21: [K3 CC, m1l CC, k1 CC, k2 MC, p1 MC, k1 MC, p1 MC, *(k1 MC, p1 MC) twice, k2 mc, k5 CC, k2 MC, p1 MC, k1 MC, p1 MC; repeat from * to 7 sts before m, (k1 MC, p1 MC) twice, k2 MC, k1 CC, m1r CC] twice, k3 CC. [327 sts]

Row 22: K3 CC, [p1 CC, (p1 MC, k1 MC) 3 times, p1, *(k1 MC, p1 MC) 3 times, p3 CC, (p1 MC, k1 MC) 3 times, p1 MC; repeat from * to 7 sts before m, (k1 MC, p1 MC) 3 times, p4 CC] twice; on the last repeat, end p1 CC, k3 CC.

Cut CC.

WITH MC:
Row 23: [K3, m1l, k2, (p1, k1) twice, p1, *(k1, p1) 3 times, k5, (p1, k1) twice, p1; repeat from * to 8 sts before m, (k1, p1) 3 times, k2, m1r] twice, k3. [331 sts]

Row 24: (K3, *p1, k1; repeat from * to 1 st before m, p4) twice; on the last repeat, end p1, k3 instead of p4.

Row 25: (K3, m1l, *k1, p1; repeat from * to 1 st before m, k1, m1r) twice, k3. [335 sts]

Row 26: (K3, *k1, p1; repeat from * to 1 st before m, k1, p3) twice; on the last repeat, end k3 instead of p3.

Row 27: (K3, m1l, *p1, k1; repeat from * to 1 st before m, p1, m1r) twice, k3. [339 sts]

Row 28: Repeat row 24.

Stitch count: 339 sts (3 border sts, 165 wing sts, 3 middle sts, 165 wing sts, 3 border sts)

BORDER SECTION CHART INSTRUCTIONS
The Border Chart (page 43) is worked twice on each row: once after the first garter edge to the middle stitches, and once more after the middle stitches to the last garter edge. Work the same row of the chart on both sides of the shawl.

The garter edge and middle stitches are worked with CC on rows 9–22 and with MC on rows 1–8 and 23–28.

Cut CC after row 1 and row 22. Cut MC after row 9.

Starting at row 1 of the Border Chart and working your way to the end of the chart, work all 28 rows the following way:

RS row: K3, sm, work from Border Chart to next m, sm, k3, sm, work same row of chart to next m, sm, k3. [4 sts inc'd]

WS row: K3, sm, work from Border Chart to next m, sm, p3, sm, work same row of chart to next m, sm, k3.

Stitch count: 339 sts (3 border sts, 165 wing sts, 3 middle sts, 165 wing sts, 3 border sts)

FINISHING
Remove markers and BO all sts in pattern. Weave in all ends and block to desired dimensions. Add tassels at each corner of the shawl.

CHART KEY

	color A
	color B
	RS: knit / WS: purl
•	RS: purl / WS: knit
/	RS: k2tog / WS: p2tog
\	RS: ssk / WS: ssp
O	yo
Ʀ	RS: m1r
Ϗ	RS: m1l
◍	bobble
	no stitch
	repeat

[continued]

TOP CHART

BODY CHART

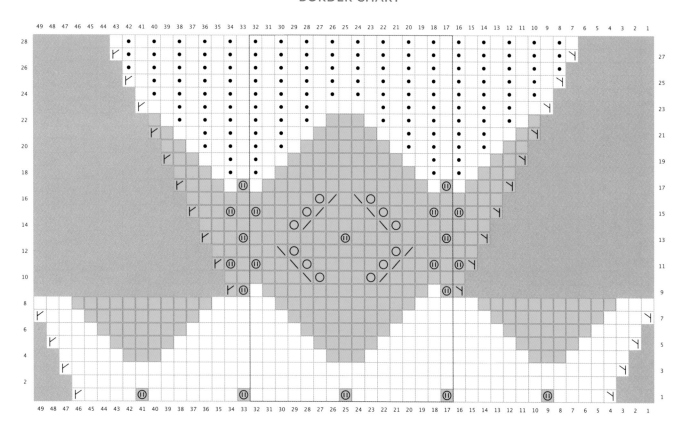

BORDER CHART

Feather Hat

I love to pay attention to the beauty of nature in the details of even its smallest elements. Feathers are a great example of subtle, natural perfection. Lighter than air but surprisingly strong, they keep the birds warm and make it possible for them to fly. As an added bonus, birds' plumages are incredibly beautiful.

This pattern comes from my desire to own a knitted plumage of my own. To create it, I observed feathers and played with lace stitches until the pattern resembled my winged friends' assets. The hat is made of several "feathers" worked side by side. Each of them starts as a large pattern and narrows toward the top of the hat. At this point, the distinction between feathers fades away to form a flower on the back of your head. The double ribbing made from a provisional cast-on makes a neat finishing and adds some extra warmth to this openwork pattern.

Construction

This hat is worked in the round from the bottom up, starting with a provisional cast-on that is undone once the ribbing is completed. The ribbing is then folded to create a double-layer brim. The body and the crown of the hat are worked in a lace pattern.

Skill Level: Intermediate

Sizes

- Child (Adult S, Adult L)

Finished Measurements

- **Brim circumference:** 17.75 (20.25, 23) inches / 45 (51, 58.5) cm
- **Recommended ease:** To be worn with approximately 1 inch (2.5 cm) of negative ease at the brim.

[continued]

Materials

YARN
DK weight, SweetGeorgia Superwash DK (100% superwash merino), 256 yds (234 m) per 115-g skein

YARDAGE/METERAGE
149 (194, 244) yds / 136 (177, 223) m

SHOWN IN
Slate (1 skein)

Any DK weight yarn can be used for this pattern. I recommend using a soft fiber that won't be itchy.

NEEDLES
For brim: US 4 (3.5 mm), 16-inch (40-cm) circular needles or DPNs, or two sizes down from needle you make gauge with

For body and crown: US 6 (4 mm), 16-inch (40-cm) circular needles or DPNs, or size needed to obtain gauge

NOTIONS
1 stitch marker
Tapestry needle
Waste yarn
Crochet hook

Gauge
22 sts × 28 rounds = 4 inches (10 cm) in lace pattern in the round using larger needle (blocked)
22 sts × 28 rounds = 4 inches (10 cm) in rib pattern in the round using smaller needle (blocked)

Special Techniques
Crochet Provisional Cast-On (page 150)

ABBREVIATIONS

CO	cast on
inc	increase
k	knit
k2tog	knit two together
k3tog	knit three together
m1l	make one left
p	purl
pm	place marker
prov CO	provisional cast-on
rem	remaining
rnd(s)	round(s)
ssk	slip slip knit
sssk	slip slip slip knit
st(s)	stitch(es)
tbl	through back loop
yo	yarn over

Feather Hat Pattern

You may work this hat either from the chart (page 47) or from the written instructions. Look for the separate sections as you proceed through the pattern.

With smaller needles and waste yarn, CO 98 (112, 126) sts using the Crochet Provisional Cast-On.

Join live yarn and knit all sts for 1 row. Pm and join to work in the round, being careful not to twist your stitches.

BRIM

Work in (p1, k1) ribbing until the brim measures 3 inches (7.5 cm).

Fold the brim inward, placing the CO edge inside and lining up the CO sts with the sts that are on the needles.

Undo your prov CO one stitch at a time, and knit together the next stitch on the needle with the stitch released from the prov CO.

Switch to larger needles.

Inc rnd: (P1, k6, m1l, k7, m1l) around. [112 (128, 144) sts]

BODY

You will now begin working from the chart (page 47), working rnds 1–8, 2 (3, 4) times [16 (24, 32) rnds total], then rnds 9–33, 1 time. [14 (16, 18) sts]

If you wish, you may use the following written instructions instead. Then proceed to **Finishing** (page 47).

Rnd 1: [P1, (k2tog, k1, yo, k1) twice, yo, k1, ssk, k1, yo, k1, ssk] around.

Rnd 2: (P1, k15) around.

Rnd 3: (P1, yo, ssk, k1, k2tog, k1, yo, k3, yo, k1, ssk, k1, k2tog, yo) around.

Rnd 4: (P2, k13, p1) around.

Rnd 5: (P2, yo, k3tog, k1, yo, k5, yo, k1, sssk, yo, p1) around.

Rnd 6: Repeat rnd 4.

Rnd 7: (P2, k2tog, k1, yo, k7, yo, k1, ssk, p1) around.

Rnd 8: Repeat rnd 4.

Work rnds 1–8, 2 (3, 4) times [16 (24, 32) rnds total].

Rnd 9: (P1, k2tog, k1, yo, k2, k2tog, yo, p1, yo, ssk, k2, yo, k1, ssk) around.

Rnd 10: (P1, k4, k2tog, yo, k1, p1, k1, yo, ssk, k4) around.

Rnd 11: (P1, k3, k2tog, yo, k2, p1, k2, yo, ssk, k3) around.

Rnd 12: (P1, k2, k2tog, yo, k3, p1, k3, yo, ssk, k2) around.

Rnd 13: (P1, k1, k2tog, yo, k2, k2tog, yo, p1, yo, ssk, k2, yo, ssk, k1) around.

Rnd 14: (P1, k2tog, yo, k2, k2tog, yo, k1, p1, k1, yo, ssk, k2, yo, ssk) around.

Rnds 15–18: Repeat rnds 11–14.

Rnd 19: [P1, k3, k2tog, yo, (p1, k tbl) twice, p1, yo, ssk, k3] around.

Rnd 20: [P1, k2, k2tog, yo, k1, (p1, k tbl) twice, p1, k1, yo, ssk, k2] around.

Rnd 21: [P1, k1, k2tog, yo, (p1, k tbl) 4 times, p1, yo, ssk, k1] around.

Rnd 22: [P1, k2tog, yo, k1, (p1, k tbl) 4 times, p1, k1, yo, ssk] around.

Rnds 23–28: (P1, k tbl) around.

Rnd 29: [(P1, k tbl) 3 times, k2tog, p1, ssk, (k tbl, p1) twice, k tbl] around. [98 (112, 126) sts]

Rnd 30: (P1, k tbl) twice, p1, k2tog, p1, ssk, (p1, k tbl) twice. [84 (96, 108) sts]

Rnd 31: (P1, k tbl) twice, k2tog, p1, ssk, k tbl, p1, k tbl. [70 (80, 90) sts]

Rnd 32: P1, k tbl, p1, k2tog, p1, ssk, p1, k tbl. [56 (64, 72) sts]

Rnd 33: P1, k tbl, k2tog, p1, ssk, k tbl. [42 (48, 54) sts]

Rnd 34: P1, k2tog, p1, ssk. [28 (32, 36) sts]

Rnd 35: P1, k3tog. [14 (16, 18) sts]

Next rnd: K2tog around. [7 (8, 9) sts]

Next rnd: K2tog to last 1 (0, 1) st, k 1 (0, 1). [4 (4, 5) sts]

FINISHING

Cut yarn, then thread through rem sts. Weave in all ends and block your hat to the desired dimensions.

CHART KEY

	knit
•	purl
/	k2tog
\	ssk
⋏	k3tog
O	yo
λ	sssk
Ω	k tbl
▓	no stitch
☐	repeat

CHART

Woodland Socks

These Woodland Socks are very cozy and warm. I love wearing them when I take a long walk in the woods or when I'm in the mood for some winter cocooning. They are made of DK weight yarn, giving them extra sturdiness to face the elements and any wear. If typical lace patterns should always use yarn overs, I'm bending the rules with this pattern, as an openwork design wouldn't be as warm. But even in this bulkier nonstandard use of lace, you will find that none of the classic lacy elegance is lost.

Construction

These socks are worked from the cuff down, the cuff coming first, followed by the leg. Both are worked in the round. Afterward, the heel flap and heel turn are worked flat. Stitches are picked up along the edges of the flap to form the gusset, which is worked in the round, followed by the foot and the toes. Stitches are then grafted together to close the sock. The stitch pattern is worked on the cuff and on the top of the foot. The final pattern is slightly different, to smoothly finish the design.

Skill Level: Intermediate

Size

- One size for adults

Finished Measurements

- **Finished leg circumference:** 8 inches / 20.25 cm, blocked

- Because of the large number of stitches used in the stitch pattern, only one size is provided. Using a slightly different gauge to achieve different measurements is encouraged. For more information, read the tips about gauge on page 17.

Materials

YARN
DK weight, Berroco Vintage® DK (52% acrylic; 40% wool; 8% nylon), 290 yds (265 m) per 100-g skein

YARDAGE/METERAGE
211 yds / 193 m

SHOWN IN
Oats 2105 (1 skein)

NEEDLES
For ribbing: US 4 (3.5 mm), DPNs, 32-inch (80-cm) circular needle for magic loop, 2 circulars or 9-inch (23-cm) circular needle

For body of sock: US 6 (4 mm), DPNs, 32-inch (80-cm) circular needle for magic loop, 2 circulars or 9-inch (23-cm) circular needle

NOTIONS
3 stitch markers
Tapestry needle

(continued)

Gauge

24 sts × 28 rows = 4 inches (10 cm) in lace pattern (blocked), with larger needles

28 sts × 30 rows = 4 inches (10 cm) in (k1, p1) ribbing (blocked), with smaller needles

Important note: Take time to check your gauge. This will ensure correct fit and yarn quantity. You can use a slightly different gauge to achieve a different size, but please do so with care and note that this will affect the required yardage.

Special Techniques

German Twisted Cast-On (page 149)

Kitchener Stitch (page 153)

ABBREVIATIONS

BOR	beginning of round
CO	cast on
dec'd	decreased
k	knit
k2tog	knit two together
m	marker
m1r	make one right
m1l	make one left
p	purl
p2tog	purl two together
pm	place marker
rem	remaining
rnd(s)	round(s)
RS	right side
sl	slip
sm	slip marker
ssk	slip slip knit
st(s)	stitch(es)
WS	wrong side
wyif	with yarn in front

Stitch Patterns

LACE PATTERN

Rnd 1: K1, m1l, ssk, k4, k2tog, k3, m1r, k1, m1l, k3, ssk, k4, k2tog, m1r.

Rnd 2 and all even-numbered rnds: K all sts.

Rnd 3: K1, m1l, k1, ssk, k2, k2tog, k4, m1r, k1, m1l, k4, ssk, k2, k2tog, k1, m1r.

Rnd 5: K1, m1l, k2, ssk, k2tog, k5, m1r, k1, m1l, k5, ssk, k2tog, k2, m1r.

Rnd 7: K1, m1l, k3, ssk, k4, k2tog, m1r, k1, m1l, ssk, k4, k2tog, k3, m1r.

Rnd 9: K1, m1l, k4, ssk, k2, k2tog, k1, m1r, k1, m1l, k1, ssk, k2, k2tog, k4, m1r.

Rnd 11: K1, m1l, k5, ssk, k2tog, k2, m1r, k1, m1l, k2, ssk, k2tog, k5, m1r.

Rnd 12: K all sts.

FINAL PATTERN

Rnd 1: K1, m1l, ssk, k4, k2tog, k3, m1r, k1, m1l, k3, ssk, k4, k2tog, m1r.

Rnd 2 and all even-numbered rnds: K all sts.

Rnd 3: K1, m1l, k1, ssk, k2, k2tog, k4, m1r, k1, m1l, k4, ssk, k2, k2tog, k1, m1r.

Rnd 5: K1, m1l, k2, ssk, k2tog, k5, m1r, k1, m1l, k5, ssk, k2tog, k2, m1r.

Rnd 7: K1, m1l, k3, ssk, k13, k2tog, k3, m1r.

Rnd 9: K1, m1l, k4, ssk, k11, k2tog, k4, m1r.

Rnd 11: K1, m1l, k5, ssk, k9, k2tog, k5, m1r.

Rnd 13: K1, m1l, k6, ssk, k7, k2tog, k6, m1r.

Rnd 15: K1, m1l, k7, ssk, k5, k2tog, k7, m1r.

Rnd 17: K1, m1l, k8, ssk, k3, k2tog, k8, m1r.

Rnd 19: K1, m1l, k9, ssk, k1, k2tog, k9, m1r.

Woodland Socks Pattern

Both socks are worked alike. You may choose to work the lace patterns from the charts (page 53) or the preceding written text.

CUFF

With smaller needles, using the German Twisted Cast-On, CO 48 sts. Pm and join to work in the round.

Work in (k1, p1) ribbing for 1 inch (2.5 cm). Switch to larger needles.

Setup rnd: K all sts.

LEG

Work the Lace Pattern twice on each rnd, working rnds 1–12 twice and rnds 1–11 once more (35 rows total).

HEEL FLAP

Remove m and place the first 24 sts on one needle. The heel flap will be worked back and forth in rows on these sts. The rem 24 sts will be worked later for the instep.

Heel flap row (RS): Sl1, (k1, sl1) to last st, k1.

Heel flap row (WS): Sl1 wyif, p to end.

Work 24 heel flap rows total.

HEEL TURN

Work the short rows as follows:

Short row 1 (RS): Sl1, k14, ssk, k1, turn work. [1 st dec'd]

Short row 2 (WS): Sl1, p7, p2tog, p1, turn work. [1 st dec'd]

Short row 3: Sl1, k to 1 st before the gap, ssk, k1, turn work. [1 st dec'd]

Short row 4: Sl1, p to 1 st before the gap, p2tog, p1, turn work. [1 st dec'd]

Repeat short rows 3–4 until all sts have been worked, 16 sts remain.

Next row (RS): K all heel sts.

GUSSET

Setup row: Pick up and k 12 sts along the edge of heel flap, pm, k24 from holder, pm, pick up and k 12 sts along heel flap, k8, pm to indicate BOR (located at the center of the heel). [64 sts]

Start working in the round.

Start working from Lace Pattern at rnd 1. The Lace Pattern is worked over the instep sts only.

Rnd 1: K to m, work next rnd of Lace Pattern over 24 sts, k to end.

Rnd 2: K to 3 sts before m, k2tog, k1, sm, work next rnd of Lace Pattern over 24 sts, sm, k1, ssk, k to end. [2 sts dec'd]

Work rnds 1–2 a total of 8 times (16 rnds total). [48 sts]

[continued]

FOOT

Foot rnd: K to m, work next rnd of Lace Pattern over 24 sts, k to end.

Work foot rnd until piece measures approximately 5.5 inches (14 cm) from back of heel or 4 inches (10 cm) shorter than the desired finished length, ending with rnd 12 of Lace Pattern.

End of foot rnd: K to m, work from Final Pattern over 24 sts, k to end.

Work the whole Final Pattern once, working a total of 19 end of foot rnds.

SHAPING TOES

Setup rnd: K9, k2tog, k1, sm, k1, ssk, k18, k2tog, k1, sm, k1, ssk, k to end. [44 sts]

Toe rnd 1: K all sts.

Toe rnd 2: (K to 3 sts before marker, k2tog, k1, sm, k1, ssk) twice, k to end. [4 sts dec'd]

Work toe rnds 1–2, 5 times total (10 rnds total). [24 sts]

Next row: K first 6 sts only.

FINISHING

Cut yarn, leaving a 12-inch (30-cm) tail.

Place the first 12 sts on one needle and the last 12 sts on a second needle. Use the Kitchener stitch to graft the toe sts.

Weave in all ends. Block to the desired dimensions.

CHART KEY

	knit
ʀ	m1r
ᴎ	m1l
╲	ssk
╱	k2tog

LACE PATTERN CHART

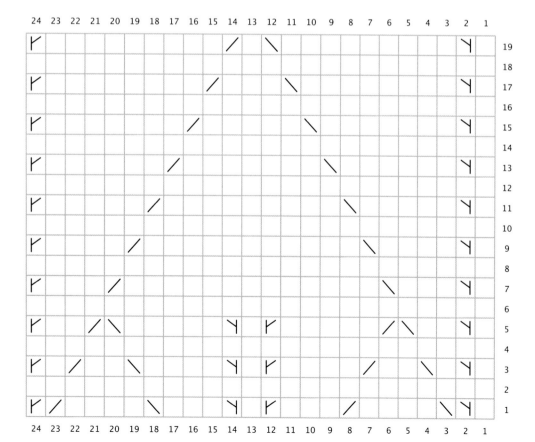

FINAL PATTERN CHART

The Hazy Collection

Fuzzy and Dainty Designs to Keep You Cozy

Misty mornings, with their smell of cool dew and their blurred scenery, are perfect peaceful moments when everything—the grass, the sky, the animals—seems to be resting in the stillness. When these moments happen, I can't resist going outside to stop for a minute or even for an hour to just breathe. The fog seems to embrace me, filling me with comfort and serenity and triggering a feeling of relaxation and happiness.

For each pattern in this chapter, I tried to capture a soft, hazy feeling. I used fuzzy yarns from hairy animals—a strand of mohair for the Samara Cardigan (page 57), a delightful baby llama yarn for the Cedar Hat and Cedar Mittens (pages 73 and 76) and alpaca yarn for the Winter Wheat Scarf (page 67). Using such yarns will create a halo of softness on your projects. However, these pieces will still turn out great even if you decide to use yarns that aren't as fuzzy—just be sure to obtain the correct gauge.

Samara Cardigan

Samara is my favorite wardrobe staple. It's easy to wear over a T-shirt, with jeans or over a dress. It keeps me warm when it's cold outside—during spring and autumn days, I can wear it instead of a jacket. It's also incredibly cozy, and because I made mine with merino wool knit together with a strand of mohair, it has an incredibly soft texture. And there's more: It looks good! When it's open, it flows around the body smoothly. When it's fastened, it has a flattering fit, with a soft V-shaped opening, some positive ease around the bust and arms, subtle waist shaping and a little more ease around the hips. The front is embellished by a lace pattern that reminds me of samaras, those little flying seeds that are just one more expression of the perfection of nature. This lace pattern, which is surprisingly easy to knit, is placed at the front, forming lace panels at each side of the opening. I bet that Samara will become one of your favorite garments too!

Construction

This cardigan is worked seamlessly from the top down. The back collar is worked first, and stitches are picked up along its edge. Raglan shaping starts from those stitches—you'll be working the fronts, sleeves and back at the same time. The lace panels are introduced progressively until they have achieved their whole width and continue on the body. When the raglan shaping is done, the sleeve stitches are put on hold and the body is worked in one piece. Waist shaping and buttonholes are worked while knitting the body, which ends with a long section of ribbing. The sleeve stitches are then put back on the needles. They are worked in the round, with decreases evenly spaced to achieve the proper wrist circumference, where a ribbed cuff is worked.

Skill Level: Intermediate

Sizes

- 1 (2, 3, 4, 5) (6, 7, 8) (9, 10, 11, 12)

Finished Measurements

- **Finished bust:** 39.25 (40.75, 43.25, 45, 47) (49.5, 53, 55.75) (59.25, 62, 64.75, 68.25) inches / 99.5 (103.5, 110, 114.5, 119.5) (125.5, 134.5, 141.5) (150.5, 157.5, 164.5, 173.5) cm

- **Recommended ease:** To be worn with approximately 4 to 8 inches (10 to 20 cm) of positive ease. Pick a size larger than your bust circumference. Sample shown is knit in size 1, worn with 5.25 inches (13.5 cm) of ease.

Materials

YARN

One strand of sport weight and one strand of laceweight mohair are held together in this sweater.

Sport weight, Malabrigo Arroyo (100% merino wool), 335 yds (306 m) per 100-g skein

Laceweight, Valley Yarns Southampton (72% mohair; 28% silk), 230 yds (210 m) per 25-g skein

YARDAGE / METERAGE OF EACH YARN

1032 (1075, 1159, 1225, 1271) (1362, 1485, 1606) (1723, 1840, 1929, 2029) yds / 944 (983, 1060, 1120, 1162) (1245, 1358, 1469) (1576, 1682, 1764, 1855) m

(continued)

SHOWN IN

Malabrigo Arroyo Sand Bank [4 (4, 4, 4, 4) (5, 5, 5) (6, 6, 6, 7) skeins]

Valley Yarns Southampton Mauve [5 (5, 6, 6, 6) (6, 7, 7) (8, 8, 9, 9) balls]

The same gauge can be achieved with one strand of worsted weight yarn.

NEEDLES

For body: US 6 (4 mm), 24- to 32-inch (60- to 80-cm) circular needle

For sleeves: US 6 (4 mm), 12-inch (30-cm) circular needle or DPNs

For neckband: US 6 (4 mm) straight or circular needle

NOTIONS

12 stitch markers

Tapestry needle

2 stitch holders or waste yarn

5–12 buttons 0.5–1 inch (1–2.5 cm) in diameter

5–12 removable markers (to indicate buttonhole placements)

Gauge

18 sts × 26 rows = 4 inches (10 cm) in stockinette stitch (blocked)

Important note: Take time to check your gauge. This will ensure correct fit and yarn quantity.

ABBREVIATIONS	
BO	bind off
CO	cast on
dec('d)	decrease(d)
inc('d)	increase(d)
k	knit
k2tog	knit two together
m	marker
m1l	make one left
m1lp	make one left purl
m1r	make one right
m1rp	make one right purl
p	purl
pm	place marker
rm	remove marker
rnd(s)	round(s)
RS	right side
sl	slip
sm	slip marker
ssk	slip slip knit
st(s)	stitch(es)
WS	wrong side
yo	yarn over

Stitch Patterns

INTRO LEFT

Row 1 (RS): M1l, yo, ssk.

Row 2 and all WS rows: P all sts.

Row 3: M1l, yo, k1, ssk.

Row 5: M1l, k2, yo, ssk.

Row 7: M1l, k2, yo, k1, ssk.

Row 9: M1l, k4, yo, ssk.

Row 11: M1l, k4, yo, k1, ssk.

Row 13: M1l, k1, k2tog, k2, yo, k1, yo, ssk.

Row 15: M1l, k1, k2tog, k2, (yo, k1) twice, ssk.

Row 17: M1l, k3, k2tog, k2, yo, k1, yo, ssk.

Row 19: M1l, k3, k2tog, k2, (yo, k1) twice, ssk.

Row 21: M1l, k1, yo, k2, ssk, k2tog, k2, yo, k1, yo, ssk.

Row 23: M1l, k1, yo, k2, ssk, k2tog, k2, (yo, k1) twice, ssk.

Row 25: M1l, k3, yo, k2, ssk, k2tog, k2, yo, k1, yo, ssk.

INTRO RIGHT

Row 1 (RS): K2tog, yo, m1r.

Row 2 and all WS rows: P all sts.

Row 3: K2tog, k1, yo, m1r.

Row 5: K2tog, yo, k2, m1r.

Row 7: K2tog, k1, yo, k2, m1r.

Row 9: K2tog, yo, k4, m1r.

Row 11: K2tog, k1, yo, k4, m1r.

Row 13: K2tog, yo, k1, yo, k2, ssk, k1, m1r.

Row 15: K2tog, (k1, yo) twice, k2, ssk, k1, m1r.

Row 17: K2tog, yo, k1, yo, k2, ssk, k3, m1r.

Row 19: K2tog, (k1, yo) twice, k2, ssk, k3, m1r.

Row 21: K2tog, yo, k1, yo, k2, ssk, k2tog, k2, yo, k1, m1r.

Row 23: K2tog, (k1, yo) twice, k2, ssk, k2tog, k2, yo, k1, m1r.

Row 25: K2tog, yo, k1, yo, k2, ssk, k2tog, k2, yo, k3, m1r.

MAIN LEFT

Row 1 (RS): K2tog, yo, k1, yo, k2, ssk, k2tog, k2, (yo, k1) twice, ssk.

Row 2 (WS): P all sts.

Row 3: K2tog, (k1, yo) twice, k2, ssk, k2tog, k2, yo, k1, yo, ssk.

Row 4: P all sts.

MAIN RIGHT

Row 1 (RS): K2tog, (k1, yo) twice, k2, ssk, k2tog, k2, yo, k1, yo, ssk.

Row 2 (WS): P all sts.

Row 3: K2tog, yo, k1, yo, k2, ssk, k2tog, k2, (yo, k1) twice, ssk.

Row 4: P all sts.

[continued]

Samara Cardigan Pattern

You may choose to work the lace patterns from the charts (page 66) or the written instructions.

- -

Note: Left and right indications refer to the wearer's side.

- -

NECKBAND SETUP

CO 12 sts.

Neckband row (left side): (P1, k1) over all sts.

Work in neckband row for 28 (28, 32, 30, 34) (36, 40, 48) (50, 50, 50, 48) rows, total.

Place sts on holder, cut yarn.

Pick up and k 12 sts from CO edge.

Neckband row (right side): (K1, p1) over all sts.

Starting with a WS row, work in neckband row for 27 (27, 31, 29, 33) (35, 39, 47) (49, 49, 49, 47) rows, total.

BODY SETUP

SETUP ROW 1 (RS)

(K1, p1) 6 times, pm, turn work so the long edge is on the top, pick up and k 53 (55, 63, 59, 67) (69, 77, 93) (99, 99, 97, 93) sts along the edge of neckband, pm, put 12 sts back from holder to live needle, (p1, k1) to end. [77 (79, 87, 83, 91) (93, 101, 117) (123, 123, 121, 117) sts]

SETUP ROW 2 (WS)

Right front: (P1, k1) 6 times, sm, p 2 (2, 2, 2, 2) (4, 4, 4) (4, 4, 4, 4), pm, p2, pm.

Right sleeve: P 10 (10, 12, 10, 12) (10, 12, 18) (22, 22, 20, 18).

Back: Pm, p2, pm, p 21 (23, 27, 27, 31) (33, 37, 41) (39, 39, 41, 41), pm, p2, pm.

Left sleeve: P 10 (10, 12, 10, 12) (10, 12, 18) (22, 22, 20, 18).

Left front: Pm, p2, pm, p 2 (2, 2, 2, 2) (4, 4, 4) (4, 4, 4, 4), sm, (k1, p1) to end.

SETUP ROW 3 (RS)

(K1, p1) 6 times, sm, m1l, k1, p1, pm, k 0 (0, 0, 0, 0) (2, 2, 2) (2, 2, 2, 2), m1r, (sm, k2, sm, m1l, k to next m, m1r) 3 times, sm, k2, sm, m1l, k 0 (0, 0, 0, 0) (2, 2, 2) (2, 2, 2, 2), pm, p1, k1, m1r, sm, (p1, k1) to end. [87 (89, 97, 93, 101) (103, 111, 127) (133, 133, 131, 127) sts]

SETUP ROW 4 (WS)

(P1, k1) 6 times, sm, p2, k1, sm, (p to next m, sm) 9 times, k1, p2, sm, (k1, p1) to end.

RAGLAN SHAPING

The raglan is shaped by completing steps with different increase rates. Work only the following steps, according to your size:

Size 1: Steps 1, 4

Size 2: Steps 1, 3, 4, 6

Sizes 3, 4, 5, 6: Steps 1, 3, 4

Size 7: Steps 1, 3

Size 8: Steps 1, 2, 3, 6

Sizes 9, 10, 11: Steps 1, 2, 3, 5

Size 12: Steps 1, 2, 3, 5, 6

STEP 1: ALL SIZES

On RS rows, increase as indicated on either side of each raglan seam and follow the Intro Charts (page 66) or the preceding Intro written text (page 59) to introduce the lace panels.

Step 1 RS row: (K1, p1) 6 times, sm, work Intro Left pattern, p1, sm, k to next m, m1r, (sm, k2, sm, m1l, k to next m, m1r) 3 times, sm, k2, sm, m1l, k to next m, sm, p1, work Intro Right pattern, sm, (p1, k1) to end. [8 sts inc'd]

Step 1 WS row: (P1, k1) 6 times, sm, work Intro Right pattern, k1, sm, (p to next m, sm) 9 times, k1, work Intro Left pattern, sm, (k1, p1) to end.

Work these 2 rows a total of 13 times (26 rows), until the Intro pattern has been fully worked.

STITCH COUNT

Each front (includes front bands and 2 raglan seam sts): 44 (44, 44, 44, 44) (46, 46, 46) (46, 46, 46, 46) sts

Each sleeve: 38 (38, 40, 38, 40) (38, 40, 46) (50, 50, 48, 46) sts

Back (includes 4 raglan seam sts): 53 (55, 59, 59, 63) (65, 69, 73) (71, 71, 73, 73) sts

Total: 217 (219, 227, 223, 231) (233, 241, 257) (263, 263, 261, 257) sts

Start working from the Main Left and Main Right charts (page 66) or the corresponding written text.

STEP 2: SIZES 8–12 **ONLY**
On RS rows, inc at the front and at every raglan seam only. Follow the charts or written instructions.

Note that in this step, the front increases are worked after the lace band.

Step 2 RS row: (K1, p1) 6 times, sm, work Main Left pattern, p1, sm, m1l, k to next m, m1r, (sm, k2, sm, m1l, k to next m, m1r) 3 times, sm, k2, sm, m1l, k to next m, m1r, sm, p1, work Main Right pattern, sm, (p1, k1) to end. [10 sts inc'd]

Step 2 WS row: (P1, k1) 6 times, sm, work Main Right pattern, k1, sm, (p to next m, sm) 9 times, k1, work Main Left pattern, sm, (k1, p1) to end.

Work these 2 rows a total of 0 (0, 0, 0, 0) (0, 0, 2) (5, 6, 7, 10) times, [0 (0, 0, 0, 0) (0, 0, 4) (10, 12, 14, 20) rows], ending on Main pattern row 0 (0, 0, 0, 0) (0, 0, 4) (2, 4, 2, 4).

STITCH COUNT
Each front (includes bands and 2 seam sts): 44 (44, 44, 44, 44) (46, 46, 50) (56, 58, 60, 66) sts

Each sleeve: 38 (38, 40, 38, 40) (38, 40, 50) (60, 62, 62, 66) sts

Back (includes 4 seam sts): 53 (55, 59, 59, 63) (65, 69, 77) (81, 83, 87, 93) sts

Total: 217 (219, 227, 223, 231) (233, 241, 277) (313, 323, 331, 357) sts

STEP 3: SIZES 2–12 **ONLY**
On RS rows, inc at every raglan seam. Follow the charts or written instructions.

Step 3 RS row: (K1, p1) 6 times, sm, work Main Left pattern, p1, sm, k to next m, m1r, (sm, k2, sm, m1l, k to next m, m1r) 3 times, sm, k2, sm, m1l, k to next m, sm, p1, work Main Right pattern, sm, (p1, k1) to end. [8 sts inc'd]

Step 3 WS row: (P1, k1) 6 times, sm, work Main Right pattern, k1, sm, (p to next m, sm) 9 times, k1, work Main Left pattern, sm, (k1, p1) to end.

Work these 2 rows a total of 0 (1, 6, 8, 12) (12, 18, 17) (11, 11, 12, 7) times, [0 (2, 12, 16, 24) (24, 36, 34) (22, 22, 24, 14) rows], ending on Main pattern row 0 (2, 4, 4, 4) (4, 4, 2) (4, 2, 2, 2).

STITCH COUNT
Each front (includes bands and 2 seam sts): 44 (45, 50, 52, 56) (58, 64, 67) (67, 69, 72, 73) sts

Each sleeve: 38 (40, 52, 54, 64) (62, 76, 84) (82, 84, 86, 80) sts

Back (includes 4 seam sts): 53 (57, 71, 75, 87) (89, 105, 111) (103, 105, 111, 107) sts

Total: 217 (227, 275, 287, 327) (329, 385, 413) (401, 411, 427, 413) sts

STEP 4: SIZES 1–6 **ONLY**
On **every** RS row, inc at Back and Sleeve raglan seams. On **every other** RS row, inc at Front, Back and Sleeve raglan seams. Follow the charts or written instructions.

Step 4 row 1 (RS): (K1, p1) 6 times, sm, work Main Left pattern, p1, sm, k to next m, m1r, (sm, k2, sm, m1l, k to next m, m1r) 3 times, sm, k2, sm, m1l, k to next m, sm, p1, work Main Right pattern, sm, (p1, k1) to end. [8 sts inc'd]

Step 4 row 2 (WS): (P1, k1) 6 times, sm, work Main Right pattern, k1, sm, (p to next m, sm) 9 times, k1, work Main Left pattern, sm, (k1, p1) to end.

Step 4 row 3 (RS): (K1, p1) 6 times, sm, work Main Left pattern, p1, sm, k to next m, (sm, k2, sm, m1l, k to next m, m1r) 3 times, sm, k2, sm, k to next m, sm, p1, work Main Right pattern, sm, (p1, k1) to end. [6 sts inc'd]

Step 4 row 4 (WS): (P1, k1) 6 times, sm, work Main Right pattern, k1, sm, (p to next m, sm) 9 times, k1, work Main Left pattern, sm, (k1, p1) to end.

Work step 4 rows a total of 5 (5, 3, 3, 1) (2, 0, 0) (0, 0, 0, 0) times, [20 (20, 12, 12, 4) (8, 0, 0) (0, 0, 0, 0) rows], ending on Main pattern row 4 (2, 4, 4, 4) (4, 4, 2) (4, 2, 2, 2).

[continued]

STITCH COUNT

Each front (includes bands and 2 seam sts): 49 (50, 53, 55, 57) (60, 64, 67) (67, 69, 72, 73) sts

Each sleeve: 58 (60, 64, 66, 68) (70, 76, 84) (82, 84, 86, 80) sts

Back (includes 4 seam sts): 73 (77, 83, 87, 91) (97, 105, 111) (103, 105, 111, 107) sts

Total: 287 (297, 317, 329, 341) (357, 385, 413) (401, 411, 427, 413) sts

STEP 5: SIZES 9–12 **ONLY**

On RS rows, inc at every raglan seam. On WS rows, inc. at Back raglan seams **only**. Follow the charts or written instructions.

Step 5 RS row: (K1, p1) 6 times, sm, work from Main Left pattern, p1, sm, k to next m, m1r, (sm, k2, sm, m1l, k to next m, m1r) 3 times, sm, k2, sm, m1l, k to next m, sm, p1, work from Main Right pattern, sm, (p1, k1) to end. [8 sts inc'd]

Step 5 WS row: (P1, k1) 6 times, sm, work from Main Right pattern, k1, sm, (p to next m, sm) 4 times, m1lp, p to next m, m1rp, (sm, p to next m) 4 times, k1, work from Main Left pattern, sm, (k1, p1) to end. [2 sts inc'd]

Work step 5 rows a total of 0 (0, 0, 0, 0) (0, 0, 0) (4, 5, 5, 8) times, [0 (0, 0, 0, 0) (0, 0, 0) (8, 10, 10, 16) rows], ending on Main pattern row 0 (0, 0, 0, 0) (0, 0, 0) (4, 4, 4, 2).

STITCH COUNT

Each front (includes bands and 2 seam sts): 49 (50, 53, 55) (57, 60, 64, 67) (71, 74, 77, 81) sts

Each sleeve: 58 (60, 64, 66, 68) (70, 76, 84) (90, 94, 96, 96) sts

Back (includes 4 seam sts): 73 (77, 83, 87, 91) (97, 105, 111) (119, 125, 131, 139) sts

Total: 287 (297, 317, 329, 341) (357, 385, 413) (441, 461, 477, 493) sts

STEP 6: SIZES 2, 8 AND 12 **ONLY**

Step 6 rows are worked even, without increasing. Follow the charts or written instructions.

Step 6 RS row: (K1, p1) 6 times, sm, work from Main Left pattern, p1, sm, k to next m, (sm, k2, sm, k to next m) 3 times, sm, k2, sm, k to next m, sm, p1, work from Main Right pattern, sm, (p1, k1) to end.

Step 6 WS row: (P1, k1) 6 times, sm, work from Main Right pattern, k1, sm, (p to next m, sm) 4 times, m1lp, p to next m, m1rp, (sm, p to next m) 4 times, k1, work from Main Left pattern, sm, (k1, p1) to end.

Work step 6 rows a total of 0 (1, 0, 0, 0) (0, 0, 1) (0, 0, 0, 1) time, [0 (2, 0, 0, 0) (0, 0, 2) (0, 0, 0, 2) rows], ending on Main pattern row 0 (4, 0, 0, 0) (0, 0, 4) (0, 0, 0, 4).

All Sizes

BODY

Division rows: Following the charts or written instructions, work the following rows.

DIVISION ROW (RS)

Front: (K1, p1) 6 times, sm, work from Main Left pattern, p1, sm, k to next m, rm, k2, rm;

Sleeve: Sl 58 (60, 64, 66, 68) (70, 76, 84) (90, 94, 96, 96) sts to holder, rm;

Back: CO 1 st, pm, CO 2 sts, k2, rm, k to next marker, rm, k2, rm, CO 1 st, pm, CO 2 sts;

Sleeve: Sl 58 (60, 64, 66, 68) (70, 76, 84) (90, 94, 96, 96) sts to holder, rm;

Front: K2, rm, k to next m, p1, work from Main Right pattern, sm, (p1, k1) to end

[**Live st count at bust:** 177 (183, 195, 203, 211) (223, 239, 251) (267, 279, 291, 307) sts

Division row (WS): (P1, k1) 6 times, sm, work from Main Right pattern, k1, sm, (p to 1 st before m, k1, sm) twice, p to next m, sm, k1, work from Main Left pattern, sm, (k1, p1) to end.

ESTABLISHING PATTERN

The optional Buttonholes and Waist Shaping occur **at the same time**. Please read ahead.

Body RS row: (K1, p1) 6 times, sm, work from Main Left pattern, p1, sm, (k to next m, sm, p1) 3 times, work from Main Right pattern, sm, (p1, k1) 6 times.

Body WS row: (P1, k1) 6 times, sm, work from Main Right pattern, k1, sm, (p to 1 st before m, k1, sm) twice, p to next m, k1, work from Main Left pattern, sm, (k1, p1) to end.

BUTTONHOLES (OPTIONAL)

Work as established until your work measures approximately 1 inch (2.5 cm) from the division row, then proceed to work the buttonholes, following the charts or written instructions. Note that the buttonholes are made by working (yo, k2tog) in the buttonhole rows, but those could be replaced by your favorite technique.

Buttonhole row (RS): (K1, p1) twice, k1, yo, k2tog, p1, (k1, p1) twice, sm, work from Main Left pattern, p1, sm, (k to next m, sm, p1) 3 times, work from Main Right pattern, sm, (p1, k1) 3 times, p1 and place a removable m in the st, (k1, p1) twice, k1.

Work a buttonhole row every 16 rows to the bottom of the body, ending with a buttonhole row followed by 3 regular body rows.

WAIST SHAPING

Work as established until your work measures approximately 2 inches (5 cm) from the division row.

Waist dec row (RS): (K1, p1) 6 times, sm, work Main Left pattern, p1, sm, (k to 3 sts before m, ssk, k1, sm, p1, k1, k2tog) twice, k to next m, sm, p1, work Main Right pattern, sm, (p1, k1) 6 times. [4 sts dec'd]

Work a waist dec row every 6 rows, 3 times. [165 (171, 183, 191, 199) (211, 227, 239) (255, 267, 279, 295) sts]

Work as established (without shaping) for 2 inches (5 cm).

Waist inc row (RS): (K1, p1) 6 times, sm, work Main Left pattern, p1, sm, (k to 1 st before m, m1r, k1, sm, p1, k1, m1l) twice, k to next m, sm, p1, work Main Right pattern, sm, (p1, k1) 6 times. [4 sts inc'd]

Work a waist inc row every 10 rows, 6 times. [189 (195, 207, 215, 223) (235, 251, 263) (279, 291, 303, 319) sts]

Continue working the lower body as established until body measures 15 (15, 15.25, 15.5, 15.5) (15.75, 15.75, 16) (16, 16.5, 16.5, 17) inches / 38 (38, 38.5, 39.5, 39.5) (40, 40, 40.5) (40.5, 42, 42, 43) cm from division row or 3 inches (7.5 cm) less than the desired finished length, ending with a WS row.

[continued]

Dec row (RS): (K1, p1) 6 times, sm, k15, p1, sm, [k 4 (3, 3, 4, 4) (4, 4, 5) (5, 5, 5, 6), k2tog] 4 (5, 5, 5, 5) (6, 6, 6) (6, 7, 7, 7) times, k 1 (1, 4, 1, 3) (0, 4, 1) (5, 1, 4, 1), sm, p1, [k 8 (8, 9, 7, 7) (8, 9, 7) (8, 9, 9, 8), k2tog] 8 (8, 8, 10, 10) (10, 10, 12) (12, 12, 12, 14) times, k 1 (5, 3, 5, 9) (5, 3, 11) (7, 1, 7, 7), sm, p1, [k 4 (3, 3, 4, 4) (4, 4, 5) (5, 5, 5, 6), k2tog] 4 (5, 5, 5, 5) (6, 6, 6) (6, 7, 7, 7) times, k 1 (1, 4, 1, 3) (0, 4, 1) (5, 1, 4, 1), sm, p1, k15, sm, (p1, k1) 6 times. [173 (177, 189, 195, 203) (213, 229, 239) (255, 265, 277, 291) sts]

Ribbing row (WS): (P1, k1) to last st, p1.

Ribbing row (RS): (K1, p1) to last st, k1.

Work in ribbing rows until ribbing measures 3 inches (7.5 cm), working buttonholes as established, ending with a WS row.

BO all sts in pattern.

SLEEVES (BOTH ALIKE)

Place 58 (60, 64, 66, 68) (70, 76, 84) (90, 94, 96, 96) sts from holder back on needles.

Beginning at the right side of the opening, join yarn and work as follows: Pick up and k 2 sts from the underarm seam, pm, pick up and k 2 more sts. K all sts up to the m. [62 (64, 68, 70, 72) (74, 80, 88) (94, 98, 100, 100) sts]

Start working in the round.

Setup rnd 1: K to last 3 sts, ssk, k1.

Setup rnd 2: K1, k2tog, k to end of rnd. [60 (62, 66, 68, 70) (72, 78, 86) (92, 96, 98, 98) sts]

Knit all sts for 14 (14, 11, 11, 9) (9, 8, 6) (5, 5, 5, 5) rnds.

Dec rnd: K1, k2tog, k to last 3 sts, ssk, k1. [2 sts dec'd; 58 (60, 64, 66, 68) (70, 76, 84) (90, 94, 96, 96) sts]

Keep working 14 (14, 11, 11, 9) (9, 8, 6) (5, 5, 5, 5) rnds followed by a dec rnd, 5 (5, 7, 7, 8) (8, 10, 14) (15, 16, 17, 16) more times. [48 (50, 50, 52, 52) (54, 56, 56) (60, 62, 62, 64) sts]

Work even until sleeve measures 14 (14, 14.25, 14.25, 14.5) (14.5, 14.75, 15) (15.25, 15.25, 15.5, 15.5) inches / 35.5 (35.5, 36, 36, 37) (37, 37.5, 38) (38.5, 38.5, 39.5, 39.5) cm from the underarm.

SIZES 1–5 **ONLY**

Wrist dec rnd 1: (K6, k2tog) 6 times, k 0 (2, 2, 4, 4) (-, -, -) (-, -, -, -). [42 (44, 44, 46, 46) (-, -, -) (-, -, -, -) sts]

Wrist dec rnd 2: (K5, k2tog) 6 times, k 0 (2, 2, 4, 4) (-, -, -) (-, -, -, -). [36 (38, 38, 40, 40) (-, -, -) (-, -, -, -) sts]

SIZES 6–10 **ONLY**

Wrist dec rnd 1: (K7, k2tog) 6 times, k - (-, -, -, -) (0, 2, 2) (6, 8, -, -). [- (-, -, -, -) (48, 50, 50) (54, 56, -, -) sts]

Wrist dec rnd 2: (K6, k2tog) 6 times, k - (-, -, -, -) (0, 2, 2) (6, 8, -, -). [- (-, -, -, -) (42, 44, 44) (48, 50, -, -) sts]

SIZES 11–12 **ONLY**

Wrist dec rnd 1: (K8, k2tog) 6 times, k - (-, -, -, -) (-, -, -) (-, -, 2, 4). [- (-, -, -, -) (-, -, -) (-, -, 56, 58) sts]

Wrist dec rnd 2: (K7, k2tog) 6 times, k - (-, -, -, -) (-, -, -) (-, -, 2, 4). [- (-, -, -, -) (-, -, -) (-, -, 50, 52) sts]

ALL SIZES

Work in (k1, p1) ribbing for 3 inches (7.5 cm).

BO all sts in pattern.

FINISHING

Weave in all ends. Block to the desired dimensions.

Sew a button at each removable marker on the button band, opposed to the buttonholes.

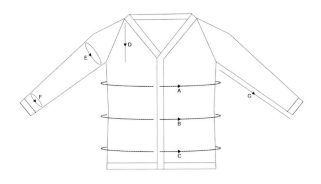

CHART KEY

	RS: knit WS: purl
O	yo
\	ssk
/	k2tog
Y	m1l
⅄	m1r
▨	no stitch

A: GARMENT WIDTH AT BUST

39.25 (40.75, 43.25, 45, 47) (49.5, 53, 55.75) (59.25, 62, 64.75, 68.25) inches

99.5 (103.5, 110, 114.5, 119.5) (125.5, 134.5, 141.5) (150.5, 157.5, 164.5, 173.5) cm

B: GARMENT WIDTH AT WAIST

36.75 (38, 40.75, 42.5, 44.25) (47, 50.5, 53) (56.75, 59.25, 62, 65.5) inches

93.5 (96.5, 103.5, 108, 112.5) (119.5, 128.5, 134.5) (144, 150.5, 157.5, 166.5) cm

C: GARMENT WIDTH AT HIPS

42 (43.25, 46, 47.75, 49.5) (52.25, 55.75, 58.5) (62, 64.75, 67.25, 71) inches

106.5 (110, 117, 121.5, 125.5) (132.5, 141.5, 148.5) (157.5, 164.5, 171, 180.5) cm

D: ARMHOLE DEPTH

7.75 (8.25, 8.25, 9, 9) (9.5, 10.25, 10.75) (10.75, 11.5, 12, 12.5) inches

19.5 (21, 21, 23, 23) (24, 26, 27.5) (27.5, 29, 30.5, 32) cm

E: SLEEVE CIRCUMFERENCE AT TOP ARM

13.75 (14.25, 15, 15.5, 16) (16.5, 17.75, 19.5) (21, 21.75, 22.25, 22.25) inches

35 (36, 38, 39.5, 40.5) (42, 45, 49.5) (53.5, 55, 56.5, 56.5) cm

F: SLEEVE CIRCUMFERENCE AT WRIST

8 (8.5, 8.5, 9, 9) (9.25, 9.75, 9.75) (10.75, 11, 11, 11.5) inches

20.5 (21.5, 21.5, 23, 23) (23.5, 25, 25) (27.5, 28, 28, 29) cm

G: SLEEVE LENGTH AT UNDERARM

17 (17, 17.25, 17.25, 17.5) (17.5, 17.75, 18) (18.25, 18.25, 18.5, 18.5) inches

43 (43, 44, 44, 44.5) (44.5, 45, 45.5) (46.5, 46.5, 47, 47) cm

[continued]

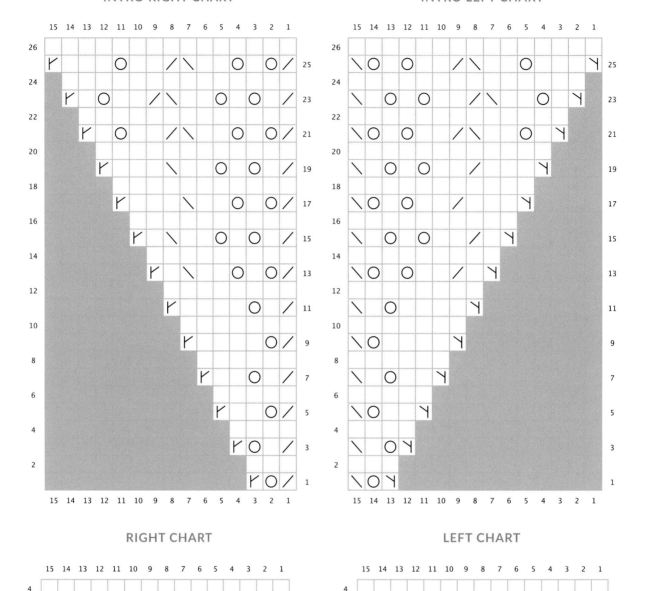

INTRO RIGHT CHART

INTRO LEFT CHART

RIGHT CHART

LEFT CHART

Winter Wheat Scarf

The Winter Wheat Scarf is a cozy accessory that you'll want to stay wrapped in during the colder months. It can be made as long and as large as desired, with my personal preference being to use as much yarn as possible, to fight the cold! This scarf has a long lace stitch pattern reminiscent of wheat stalks and is ornamented with cheerful bobbles.

Construction

This scarf is worked lengthwise, starting with a ribbing section that is broken by a lace stitch pattern. Once the ribbing is completed, the lace pattern continues and a different lace pattern is worked where there was ribbing. Once the length of the scarf is achieved, a matching ribbing section is worked on the other end.

Skill Level: Intermediate

Size

- One size for adults

Finished Measurements

- 9 inches (23 cm) wide and 100 inches (254 cm) long, blocked

Materials

YARN

Aran weight, Knit Picks® Simply Alpaca Aran (100% superfine alpaca), 246 yds (225 m) per 100-g skein

YARDAGE/METERAGE

775 yds (709 m)

SHOWN IN

Alonzo (4 skeins)

While I technically used Aran weight yarn for this project, the gauge achieved is much closer to sport weight. If you are substituting yarn and want to achieve the same gauge, I would strongly suggest using sport weight yarn. The scarf can also be made with any fingering to heavy worsted weight. Gauge, yardage and final size will vary.

NEEDLES

US 6 (4 mm) needles, or size needed to obtain gauge

Important note: Gauge can vary according to your yarn and needle size. If your gauge differs, your scarf will have different dimensions from the prototype. Make sure to plan enough yardage for the dimensions that you're expecting to reach.

NOTIONS

Tapestry needle
Crochet hook to make bobbles

(continued)

Gauge

31 sts × 23 rows = 4 inches (10 cm) in Ribbing and Lace Patterns (blocked)

Important note: Take time to check your gauge. This will ensure correct fit and yarn quantity.

Note on gauge: Gauge is taken on the whole scarf, after blocking. The weight of the scarf will have an effect on the proportions of the scarf, stretching the row gauge and reducing the stitch gauge significantly compared to a small swatch. The opposite gauge (23 sts × 31 rows) is to be expected on a small swatch (approximately).

Special Techniques

Bobbles (page 152): For this pattern, I recommend doing 4 repetitions of (k1, yo) in the same stitch.

ABBREVIATIONS	
BO	bind off
CO	cast on
k	knit
k3tog	knit three together
mb	make bobble
p	purl
RS	right side
st(s)	stitch(es)
sssk	slip slip slip knit
WS	wrong side
yo	yarn over

Winter Wheat Scarf Pattern

- -

Note: The number of stitches varies between rows. There is one less stitch for each repetition of the pattern on row 1 of the Ribbing Pattern, rows 1 and 5 of the Main Pattern and Last Lace Pattern. On the following rows, the stitch is added back. Bobbles can be omitted to create a more sober result. To do so, simply knit the stitches where the bobbles are made.

- -

SETUP

CO 71 sts (or a multiple of 20 + 11 sts).

Setup row (WS): (P1, k1) twice, [p3, (k1, p1) 8 times, k1] to last 7 sts, p3, (k1, p1) twice.

RIBBING

Work all 4 rows of Ribbing Pattern 16 times (64 rows total), following the Ribbing Chart (page 71) or the following written instructions. Then proceed to **Main Section**.

RIBBING PATTERN

Row 1 (RS): (K1, p1) twice, [k3tog, yo, (p1, k1) 8 times, p1] to last 7 sts, k3tog, yo, (p1, k1) twice. [67 sts]

Row 2 (WS): (P1, k1) twice, p1, yo, p1, [(k1, p1) 9 times, yo, p1] to last 4 sts, (k1, p1) twice. [71 sts]

Row 3: (K1, p1) twice, [k3, (p1, k1) 8 times, p1] to last 7 sts, k3, (k1, p1) twice.

Row 4: (P1, k1) twice, p3, [(k1, p1) 8 times, k1, p3] to last 4 sts, (k1, p1) twice.

MAIN SECTION

Work all 8 rows of Main Pattern 55 times (440 rows total) or any number of times, following the Main Pattern Chart (page 71) or the following written instructions. Then proceed to **Last Lace Pattern** (page 70).

[continued]

MAIN PATTERN

Row 1 (RS): (K1, p1) twice, [k3tog, yo, p1, k3tog, k3, (yo, k1) 3 times, yo, k3, sssk, p1] to last 7 sts, k3tog, yo, (p1, k1) twice. [67 sts]

Row 2 (WS): (P1, k1) twice, p1, yo, p1, (k1, p15, k1, p1, yo, p1) to last 4 sts, (k1, p1) twice. [71 sts]

Row 3: (K1, p1) twice, (k3, p1, k3tog, k2, yo, k1, yo, k3, yo, k1, yo, k2, sssk, p1) to last 7 sts, k3, (p1, k1) twice.

Row 4: (P1, k1) twice, p3, (k1, p15, k1, p3) to last 4 sts, (k1, p1) twice.

Row 5: (K1, p1) twice, [k3tog, yo, p1, k3tog, (k1, yo) twice, k2, mb, k2, (yo, k1) twice, sssk, p1] to last 7 sts, k3tog, yo, (p1, k1) twice. [67 sts]

Row 6: Repeat row 2. [71 sts]

Row 7: (K1, p1) twice, (k3, p1, k3tog, yo, k1, yo, k7, yo, k1, yo, sssk, p1) to last 7 sts, k3, (p1, k1) twice.

Row 8: Repeat row 4.

LAST LACE PATTERN

Work all 8 rows of Last Lace Pattern once, following Last Lace Pattern Chart (page 71) or the following written instructions. Then proceed to **Ribbing**.

LAST LACE PATTERN

Row 1 (RS): (K1, p1) twice, [k3tog, yo, p1, k3tog, k3, (yo, k1) 3 times, yo, k3, sssk, p1] to last 7 sts, k3tog, yo, (p1, k1) twice. [67 sts]

Row 2 (WS): (P1, k1) twice, p1, yo, p1, [(k1, p7) twice, k1, p1, yo, p1] to last 4 sts, (k1, p1) twice. [71 sts]

Row 3: (K1, p1) twice, [k3, p1, k3tog, k2, (yo, k1) twice, p1, (k1, yo) twice, k2, sssk, p1] to last 7 sts, k3, (p1, k1) twice.

Row 4: (P1, k1) twice, p3, [k1, p5, (k1, p1) twice, k1, p5, k1, p3] to last 4 sts, (k1, p1) twice.

Row 5: (K1, p1) twice, [k3tog, yo, p1, k3tog, (k1, yo) twice, (p1, k1) twice, p1, (yo, k1) twice, sssk, p1] to last 7 sts, k3tog, yo, (p1, k1) twice. [67 sts]

Row 6: (P1, k1) twice, p1, yo, p1, [k1, p5, (k1, p1) twice, k1, p5, k1, p1, yo, p1] to last 4 sts, (k1, p1) twice. [71 sts]

Row 7: (K1, p1) twice, [k3, p1, k3tog, yo, k1, yo, (k1, p1) 3 times, (k1, yo) twice, sssk, p1] to last 7 sts, k3, (p1, k1) twice.

Row 8: (P1, k1) twice, p3, [(k1, p1) 8 times, k1, p3] to last 4 sts, (k1, p1) twice.

RIBBING

Work all 4 rows of Ribbing Pattern 16 times (64 rows total), following Ribbing Chart (page 71) or the following written instructions. Then proceed to **Finishing**.

RIBBING PATTERN

Row 1 (RS): (K1, p1) twice, [k3tog, yo, (p1, k1) 8 times, p1] to last 7 sts, k3tog, yo, (p1, k1) twice. [67 sts]

Row 2 (WS): (P1, k1) twice, p1, yo, p1, [(k1, p1) 9 times, yo, p1] to last 4 sts, (k1, p1) twice. [71 sts]

Row 3: (K1, p1) twice, [k3, (p1, k1) 8 times, p1] to last 7 sts, k3, (p1, k1) twice.

Row 4: (P1, k1) twice, p3, [(k1, p1) 8 times, k1, p3] to last 4 sts, (k1, p1) twice.

FINISHING

BO all sts. Cut yarn and weave in all ends. Block your scarf to the desired dimensions.

CHART KEY

	RS: knit WS: purl
⅄	k3tog
⅄	sssk
O	yo
⑩	bobble
·	RS: purl WS: knit
▓	no stitch
	repeat

RIBBING CHART

| 31 | 30 | 29 | 28 | 27 | 26 | 25 | 24 | 23 | 22 | 21 | 20 | 19 | 18 | 17 | 16 | 15 | 14 | 13 | 12 | 11 | 10 | 9 | 8 | 7 | 6 | 5 | 4 | 3 | 2 | 1 |

MAIN PATTERN CHART

| 31 | 30 | 29 | 28 | 27 | 26 | 25 | 24 | 23 | 22 | 21 | 20 | 19 | 18 | 17 | 16 | 15 | 14 | 13 | 12 | 11 | 10 | 9 | 8 | 7 | 6 | 5 | 4 | 3 | 2 | 1 |

LAST LACE PATTERN CHART

| 31 | 30 | 29 | 28 | 27 | 26 | 25 | 24 | 23 | 22 | 21 | 20 | 19 | 18 | 17 | 16 | 15 | 14 | 13 | 12 | 11 | 10 | 9 | 8 | 7 | 6 | 5 | 4 | 3 | 2 | 1 |

Cedar Hat

When the days are cold, I like to bundle up in some feel-good accessories that are both comfortable and elegant. And what's more elegant than a matching set? The Cedar Hat and Cedar Mittens (page 76) are must-have midseason accessories. This simple beanie is worked mostly in stockinette stitch. It is embellished by a lace pattern in the form of columns, reminiscent of tall cedar trees, which take root at the beginning of the ribbing.

Construction

The Cedar Hat is worked in the round, from the bottom up, starting with a brim made by alternating ribbing and lace. The lace pattern continues on the body, alternating with stockinette stitch. On the top of the hat, the lace columns are merged together, forming a star-shaped pattern at the top of the crown.

Skill Level: Advanced beginner

Sizes

- Child (Adult S, Adult L)

Finished Measurements

- **Brim circumference:** 17.5 (19.75, 21.75) inches / 44.5 (50, 55) cm

- **Recommended ease:** Pick a size 2 to 3 inches (5 to 7.5 cm) smaller than your head circumference. Sample is size adult S worn with 2 inches (5 cm) of negative ease.

Materials

YARN
DK weight, Illimani Baby Llama (100% dehaired baby llama), 220 yds (201 m) per 100-g skein

YARDAGE/METERAGE
125 (156, 181) yds / 114 (143, 166) m

SHOWN IN
Beige BC (1 skein)

NEEDLES
For brim: US 2 (2.75 mm), 16-inch (40-cm) circular needle, or two sizes smaller than the size needed to obtain gauge

For body and crown: US 4 (3.5 mm), 16-inch (40-cm) circular needle, or size needed to obtain gauge

NOTIONS
1 stitch marker
Tapestry needle

Gauge

22 sts × 28 rnds = 4 inches (10 cm) in Body pattern using larger needles (blocked)

22 sts × 28 rnds = 4 inches (10 cm) in Ribbing pattern using smaller needles (blocked)

Important note: Take time to check your gauge. This will ensure correct fit and yarn quantity.

Special Techniques
German Twisted Cast-On (page 149)

[continued]

ABBREVIATIONS	
cdd	central double decrease
CO	cast on
inc	increase
k	knit
k2tog	knit two together
k3tog	knit three together
m1l	make one left
m1r	make one right
p	purl
pm	place marker
rem	remaining
rnd(s)	round(s)
ssk	slip slip knit
sssk	slip slip slip knit
st(s)	stitch(es)
yo	yarn over

Cedar Hat Pattern

With smaller needles, using the German Twisted Cast-On, CO 96 (108, 120) sts.

Pm and join to work in the round, being careful not to twist your stitches.

- -

Note: The number of stitches in the lace sections varies from rnd to rnd. Two stitches per lace section are decreased in brim rnd 3, body rnd 1, crown setup rnd 2 and crown rnd 4. The stitches are added back in the next row.

- -

BRIM

Work 16 (20, 20) brim rnds, working the following 4 rnds 4 (5, 5) times.

Brim rnd 1: [P1, k7, (p1, k1) 4 (5, 6) times] around.

Brim rnd 2: Repeat rnd 1.

Brim rnd 3: [P1, k3tog, yo, k1, yo, sssk, (p1, k1) 4 (5, 6) times] around. [84 (96, 108) sts]

Brim rnd 4: [P1, k1, yo, k3, yo, k1, (p1, k1) 4 (5, 6) times] around. [96 (108, 120) sts]

Switch to larger needles.

Inc rnd: [P1, k7, p1, k1, m1r, k 5 (7, 9), m1l, k1] around. [108 (120, 132) sts]

Next rnd: [P1, k7, p1, k 9 (11, 13)] around.

BODY

Work 37 (40, 43) body rnds, ending with rnd 1 (4, 3).

Body rnd 1: [P1, k3tog, yo, k1, yo, sssk, p1, k 9 (11, 13)] around.

Body rnd 2: [P1, k1, yo, k3, yo, k1, p1, k 9 (11, 13)] around.

Body rnd 3: [P1, k7, p1, k 9 (11, 13)] around.

Body rnd 4: Repeat rnd 3.

Stitch count: 96 (120, 132) sts

CROWN

ADULT L ONLY
Crown setup rnd 1: (P1, k7, p1, ssk, k9, k2tog) around. [- (-), 120 sts]

ADULT S, L ONLY
Crown setup rnd 2: (P1, k3tog, yo, k1, yo, sssk, p1, ssk, k7, k2tog) around. [- (96, 96) sts]

ALL SIZES

Rnd 1: (P1, k1, yo, k3, yo, k1, p1, ssk, k5, k2tog) around. [96 sts]

Rnd 2: (P1, k7, p1, ssk, k3, k2tog) around. [84 sts]

Rnd 3: (P1, k7, p1, ssk, k1, k2tog) around. [72 sts]

Rnd 4: (P1, k3tog, yo, k1, yo, sssk, p1, cdd) around. [48 sts]

Rnd 5: (P1, k1, yo, k3, yo, k1, p1, k1) around. [60 sts]

Rnd 6: (P1, ssk, k3, k2tog, p1, k1) around. [48 sts]

Rnd 7: (P1, ssk, k1, k2tog, p1, k1) around. [36 sts]

Rnd 8: (P1, cdd, p1, k1) around. [24 sts]

Rnd 9: Ssk around. [12 sts]

Rnd 10: Ssk around. [6 sts]

Cut yarn, insert through rem sts.

Weave in all ends.

Cedar Mittens

The Cedar Mittens are a perfect match to the Cedar Hat (page 73). These mittens will give you just the right amount of extra warmth and comfort when the days get colder. They are worked simply in stockinette stitch, with the tall cedar pattern enhancing the top of the mittens, starting at the ribbing and running up to the tips of your fingers.

Construction

The Cedar Mittens are worked in the round, starting with a ribbed cuff embellished with a column of lace stitches on the top of the hand. The lace pattern continues on the mitten, which is otherwise worked in stockinette stitch. The thumb gusset is formed while knitting, and stitches are placed on hold when it's done. The palm of the mitten is then worked on the live stitches until the length is achieved, and stitches are decreased at the top. The thumb is worked afterward from the stitches put on hold.

Skill Level: Advanced beginner

Sizes

- Child (Adult S, Adult L)

Finished Measurements

- 7 (7.75, 8.5) inches / 18 (20, 22) cm of circumference at palm

- **Recommended ease:** Pick a size slightly larger than your palm circumference. Prototype is size adult S worn with approximately 0.5 inch (1.5 cm) of positive ease.

Materials

YARN
DK weight, Illimani Baby Llama (100% dehaired baby llama), 220 yds (201 m) per 100-g skein

YARDAGE/METERAGE
139 (173, 206) yds / 127 (158, 188) m

SHOWN IN
Beige BC (1 skein)

NEEDLES
For cuff: US 2 (2.75 mm), DPNs or 9- or 12-inch (23- or 30-cm) circular needles, or two sizes down from needle that you make gauge with

For mitten body: US 4 (3.5 mm), DPNs or 9- or 12-inch (23- or 30-cm) circular needles, or size needed to obtain gauge

NOTIONS
3 stitch markers
Tapestry needle

Gauge
22 sts × 28 rows = 4 inches (10 cm) in stockinette stitch using larger needle (blocked)

Important note: Take time to check your gauge. This will ensure correct fit and yarn quantity.

Special Techniques
German Twisted Cast-On (page 149)

[continued]

ABBREVIATIONS	
BOR	Beginning of round
CO	cast on
dec'd	decreased
inc'd	increased
k	knit
k2tog	knit two together
k3tog	knit three together
m	marker
m1l	make one left
m1r	make one right
p	purl
pm	place marker
rem	remaining
rm	remove marker
rnd(s)	round(s)
sm	slip marker
ssk	slip slip knit
sssk	slip slip slip knit
st(s)	stitch(es)
yo	yarn over

Cedar Mittens Pattern

- -

Note: The number of stitches in the lace sections varies from round to round. Two stitches per lace section are decreased in cuff rnd 3, setup rnd 3, thumb gusset rnds 3 and 7, palm rnd 3 and top decreases rnd 3. The stitches are added back in the next row.

- -

LEFT MITTEN

With smaller needles, CO 40 (44, 48) sts, using the German Twisted Cast-On.

Pm to indicate BOR and join to work in the round, being careful not to twist your stitches.

CUFF

Work 16 (20, 20) cuff rnds, working the following 4 rnds 4 (5, 5) times.

Rnd 1: (K1, p1) 8 (9, 10) times, k7, p1, (k1, p1) 8 (9, 10) times.

Rnd 2: Repeat rnd 1.

Rnd 3: (K1, p1) 8 (9, 10) times, k3tog, yo, k1, yo, sssk, p1, (k1, p1) 8 (9, 10) times. [38 (42, 46) sts]

Rnd 4: (K1, p1) 8 (9, 10) times, k1, yo, k3, yo, k1, p1, (k1, p1) 8 (9, 10) times. [40 (44, 48) sts]

Switch to larger needles.

SETUP

Rnd 1: K 15 (17, 19), p1, k7, p1, k 16 (18, 20).

Rnd 2: Repeat rnd 1.

Rnd 3: K 15 (17, 19), p1, k3tog, yo, k1, yo, sssk, p1, k to end.

Rnd 4: K 7 (8, 9), pm, m1l, k1, m1r, pm, k 7 (8, 9), p1, k1, yo, k3, yo, k1, p1, k 16 (18, 20). [3 sts for thumb gusset; 42 (46, 50) total sts]

THUMB GUSSET

Form the thumb gusset by working 16 (18, 21) rnds, working the following 12 rnds once and repeating rnds 1–4 (6, 9) once more.

Rnd 1: (K to next m, sm) twice, k 7 (8, 9), p1, k7, p1, k to end.

Rnd 2: Repeat rnd 1.

Rnd 3: K to marker, sm, m1l, k to next m, m1r, sm, k 7 (8, 9), p1, k3tog, yo, k1, yo, sssk, p1, k to end. [2 sts inc'd; 2 sts dec'd]

Rnd 4: (K to next m, sm) twice, k 7 (8, 9), p1, k1, yo, k3, yo, k1, p1, k to end. [2 sts inc'd]

Rnd 5: Repeat rnd 1.

Rnd 6: K to m, sm, m1l, k to next m, m1r, sm, k 7 (8, 9), p1, k7, p1, k to end. [2 sts inc'd]

Rnd 7: (K to m, sm) twice, k 7 (8, 9), p1, k3tog, yo, k1, yo, sssk, p1, k to end. [2 sts dec'd]

Rnd 8: Repeat rnd 4.

Rnd 9: Repeat rnd 6. [2 sts inc'd]

Rnd 10: Repeat rnd 1.

Rnd 11: Repeat rnd 7. [2 sts dec'd]

Rnd 12: K to m, sm, m1l, k to next m, m1r, sm, k 7 (8, 9), p1, k1, yo, k3, yo, k1, p1, k to end. [4 sts inc'd]

STITCH COUNT

Stitch count between thumb markers: 13 (15, 17) sts

Total stitch count: 52 (58, 64) sts

SEPARATING THUMB AND PALM STITCHES

Division rnd (sizes Child and Adult L only): K to m, rm, place sts between markers on waste yarn or stitch holder, rm, k 7 (-, 9), p1, k7, p1, k to end.

Division rnd (size Adult S only): K to m, rm, place sts between markers on waste yarn or stitch holder, rm, k8, p1, k3tog, yo, k1, yo, sssk, p1, k to end.

Stitch count: 39 (41, 47) sts

ALL SIZES

Move the BOR marker one stitch earlier, so the last stitch of the round is now the first stitch. There will be 15 (17, 19) k sts on both sides of the BOR marker, before the pattern.

PALM ROUNDS

Beginning with palm rnd 2 (4, 3), work palm rnds until mitten measures approximately 7.5 (8, 9) inches / 19 (20.5, 23) cm from the end of cuff or is the desired length to fit comfortably, ending with rnd 4.

Palm rnd 1: K 15 (17, 19), p1, k7, p1, k to end.

Palm rnd 2: Repeat rnd 1.

Palm rnd 3: K 15 (17, 19), p1, k3tog, yo, k1, yo, sssk, p1, k to end.

Palm rnd 4: K 15 (17, 19), p1, k1, yo, k3, yo, k1, p1, k to end.

TOP DECREASES

Rnd 1: K 5 (6, 7), k2tog, k1, ssk, k 5 (6, 7), p1, k7, p1, k 5 (6, 7), k2tog, k1, ssk, k to end. [35 (39, 43) sts]

Rnd 2: K 4 (5, 6), k2tog, k1, ssk, k 4 (5, 6), p1, k7, p1, k 4 (5, 6), k2tog, k1, ssk, k to end. [31 (35, 39) sts]

Rnd 3: K 3 (4, 5), k2tog, k1, ssk, k 3 (4, 5), p1, k3tog, yo, k1, yo, sssk, p1, k 3 (4, 5), k2tog, k1, ssk, k to end. [25 (29, 33) sts]

Rnd 4: K 2 (3, 4), k2tog, k1, ssk, k 2 (3, 4), p1, k1, yo, k3, yo, k1, p1, k 2 (3, 4), k2tog, k1, ssk, k to end. [23 (27, 31) sts]

Rnd 5: K 1 (2, 3), k2tog, k1, ssk, k 1 (2, 3), p1, k7, p1, k 1 (2, 3), k2tog, k1, ssk, k to end. [19 (23, 27) sts]

Rnd 6: K 0 (1, 2), k2tog, k1, ssk, k 0 (1, 2), p1, k7, p1, k 0 (1, 2), k2tog, k1, ssk, k to end. [15 (19, 23) sts]

Rnd 7 (size Child only): K3, p1, ssk, k3, k2tog, p1, k3. [13 (19, 23) sts]

[continued]

Rnd 7 (sizes Adult S and L only): K - (0, 1), k2tog, k1, ssk, k1, p1, ssk, k3, k2tog, p1, k - (0, 1), k2tog, k1, ssk, k to end. [13 (13, 17) sts]

Rnd 8 (sizes Child and Adult S only): K3, p1, ssk, k1, k2tog, p1, k3. [11 (11, 17) sts]

Rnd 8 (size Adult L only): K2tog, k1, ssk, p1, ssk, k1, k2tog, p1, k2tog, k1, ssk. [11 (11, 11) sts]

Cut yarn, leaving a 6-inch (15-cm) tail. Thread it through the rem sts. Pull tight to close the top of the mitten.

RIGHT MITTEN

With smaller needles, using the German Twisted Cast-On method, CO 40 (44, 48) sts.

Pm to indicate BOR and join to work in the round, being careful not to twist your stitches.

CUFF

Work 16 (20, 20) cuff rnds, working the following 4 rnds 4 (5, 5) times.

Rnd 1: (P1, k1) 8 (9, 10) times, p1, k7, (p1, k1) 8 (9, 10) times.

Rnd 2: Repeat rnd 1.

Rnd 3: (P1, k1) 8 (9, 10) times, p1, k3tog, yo, k1, yo, sssk, (p1, k1) 8 (9, 10) times.

Rnd 4: (P1, k1) 8 (9, 10) times, p1, k1, yo, k3, yo, k1, (p1, k1) 8 (9, 10) times.

Switch to larger needles.

SETUP

Rnd 1: K 16 (18, 20), p1, k7, p1, k 15 (17, 19).

Rnd 2: Repeat rnd 1.

Rnd 3: K 16 (18, 20), p1, k3tog, yo, k1, yo, sssk, p1, k to end.

Rnd 4: K 16 (18, 20), p1, k1, yo, k3, yo, k1, p1, k 7 (8, 9), pm, m1l, k1, m1r, pm, k 7 (8, 9).

THUMB GUSSET

Form the thumb gusset by working 16 (18, 21) rnds, working the following 12 rnds once and repeating rnds 1–4 (6, 9) once more.

Rnd 1: K 16 (18, 20), p1, k7, p1, (k to next m, sm) twice, k to end.

Rnd 2: Repeat rnd 1.

Rnd 3: K 16 (18, 20), p1, k3tog, yo, k1, yo, sssk, p1, k to m, sm, m1l, k to next m, m1r, sm, k to end. [2 sts inc'd; 2 sts dec'd]

Rnd 4: K 16 (18, 20), p1, k1, yo, k3, yo, k1, p1, (k to next m, sm) twice, k to end. [2 sts inc'd]

Rnd 5: Repeat rnd 1.

Rnd 6: K 16 (18, 20), p1, k7, p1, k to m, sm, m1l, k to next m, m1r, sm, k to end. [2 sts inc'd]

Rnd 7: K 16 (18, 20), p1, k3tog, yo, k1, yo, sssk, p1, (k to m, sm) twice, k to end. [2 sts dec'd]

Rnd 8: Repeat rnd 4.

Rnd 9: Repeat rnd 6. [2 sts inc'd]

Rnd 10: Repeat rnd 1.

Rnd 11: Repeat rnd 7. [2 sts dec'd]

Rnd 12: K 16 (18, 20), p1, k1, yo, k3, yo, k1, p1, k to m, sm, m1l, k to next m, m1r, sm, k to end. [4 sts inc'd]

STITCH COUNT
Stitch count between thumb markers: 13 (15, 17) sts

Total stitch count: 52 (58, 64) sts

SEPARATING THUMB AND PALM STITCHES
Division rnd (sizes Child and Adult L only): K 16 (-, 20), p1, k7, p1, k to m, rm, place sts between markers on waste yarn or stitch holder, rm, k to end.

Division rnd (size Adult S only): K18, p1, k3tog, yo, k1, yo, sssk, p1, k to m, rm, place sts between markers on waste yarn or stitch holder, rm, k to end.

Stitch count: 39 (43, 47) sts

Move the BOR marker one stitch farther, so the first stitch of the round is now the last stitch. There will be 15 (17, 19) k sts on both sides of the BOR marker, before the pattern.

PALM
Beginning with palm rnd 2 (4, 3), work palm rnds until the mitten measures approximately 7.5 (8, 9) inches / 19 (20.5, 23) cm from the end of cuff or is the desired length to fit comfortably, ending with rnd 4.

Palm rnd 1: K 15 (17, 19), p1, k7, p1, k to end.

Palm rnd 2: Repeat rnd 1.

Palm rnd 3: K 15 (17, 19), p1, k3tog, yo, k1, yo, sssk, p1, k to end.

Palm rnd 4: K 15 (17, 19), p1, k1, yo, k3, yo, k1, p1, k to end.

TOP DECREASES
Rnd 1: K 5 (6, 7), k2tog, k1, ssk, k 5 (6, 7), p1, k7, p1, k 5 (6, 7), k2tog, k1, ssk, k to end. [35 (39, 43) sts]

Rnd 2: K 4 (5, 6), k2tog, k1, ssk, k 4 (5, 6), p1, k7, p1, k 4 (5, 6), k2tog, k1, ssk, k to end. [31 (35, 39) sts]

Rnd 3: K 3 (4, 5), k2tog, k1, ssk, k 3 (4, 5), p1, k3tog, yo, k1, yo, sssk, p1, k 3 (4, 5), k2tog, k1, ssk, k to end. [25 (29, 33) sts]

Rnd 4: K 2 (3, 4), k2tog, k1, ssk, k 2 (3, 4), p1, k1, yo, k3, yo, k1, p1, k 2 (3, 4), k2tog, k1, ssk, k to end. [23 (27, 31) sts]

Rnd 5: K 1 (2, 3), k2tog, k1, ssk, k 1 (2, 3), p1, k7, p1, k 1 (2, 3), k2tog, k1, ssk, k to end. [19 (23, 27) sts]

Rnd 6: K 0 (1, 2), k2tog, k1, ssk, k 0 (1, 2), p1, k7, p1, k 0 (1, 2), k2tog, k1, ssk, k to end. [15 (19, 23) sts]

Rnd 7 (size Child only): K3, p1, ssk, k3, k2tog, p1, k3. [13 (19, 23) sts]

Rnd 7 (sizes Adult S and L only): K - (0, 1), k2tog, k1, ssk, k1, p1, ssk, k3, k2tog, p1, k - (0, 1), k2tog, k1, ssk, k to end. [13 (13, 17) sts]

Rnd 8 (sizes Child and Adult S only): K3, p1, ssk, k1, k2tog, p1, k3. [11 (11, 17) sts]

Rnd 8 (size Adult L only): K2tog, k1, ssk, p1, ssk, k1, k2tog, p1, k2tog, k1, ssk. [11 (11, 11) sts]

ALL SIZES
Cut yarn, leaving a 6-inch (15-cm) tail. Thread it through the rem sts. Pull tight to close the top of the mitten.

THUMBS (BOTH ALIKE)
Place 13 (15, 17) thumb sts on DPNs, joining yarn at the opening.

Pick up and k 1 st from the opening, k all sts, pick up and k 1 st from the opening. [15 (17, 19) sts]

Pm and join to work in the round.

K all sts until the thumb measures 2.25 (2.5, 2.75) inches / 6 (6.5, 7) cm or is the desired length to fit comfortably.

TOP DECREASES
Rnd 1: K2tog to last st, k1. [8 (9, 10) sts]

Rnd 2 (sizes Child and Adult L only): K2tog around. [4 (9, 5) sts]

Rnd 2 (size Adult S only): K2tog to last st, k1. [4 (5, 5) sts]

Cut yarn, leaving a 4-inch (10-cm) tail. Thread it through the rem sts. Pull tight to close the top of thumb.

FINISHING
Weave in all ends. Block to the desired dimensions.

The *Aerial* Collection

Romantic Patterns to Enhance Your Skills

Air is the essence of life, yet it is so subtle that we can sometimes forget its presence. It can be magical to stop the hustle and bustle for just an instant, to mindfully feel that element that we so easily take for granted. Is there a warm breeze today? Or is the air so cold that it freezes your cheeks? Or maybe air and water are dancing together and the mist feels like you're walking in a cloud?

This romantic collection of patterns has something aerial—a lightness and a flow—that gives these designs a feeling of gentle airiness. The Pinnate Tank Top (page 97), Periwinkle Shawl (page 105) and Lyrebird Socks (page 114), with their flowing lines and lighter yarns, are perfect for embracing the soothing touch of air. Meanwhile, the Amarelle Sweater (page 85) is a much warmer garment that will keep you warm even in a chilly wind.

Amarelle Sweater

Worked in worsted weight yarn and made with a circular yoke and turtleneck, Amarelle is a classic staple for comfort and warmth. The intricate lace pattern forms an interesting design reminiscent of leaves and fruits—it is just as exquisite as the sour cherries it represents.

Construction

This sweater is worked in the round from the top down, starting with a provisional cast-on, followed by a small section of short rows and a circular lace yoke. Once the yoke is completed, the stitches from the sleeves are placed on hold and the body is worked, ending with a section of ribbing. The sleeve stitches are then put back on live needles and the sleeves are worked down to the wrist, ending with another ribbing section. The provisional cast-on is then undone and the cowl is worked in even more ribbing.

Skill Level: Intermediate

Sizes

- 1 (2, 3, 4) (5, 6, 7, 8) (9, 10, 11, 12)

Finished Measurements

- **Finished bust:** 32 (34.5, 36.75, 39.25) (41.75, 44.25, 47.5, 49.75) (52.25, 54.75, 58, 61.5) inches / 81.5 (87.5, 93.5, 99.5) (106, 112.5, 120.5, 126.5) (132.5, 139, 147.5, 156) cm
- **Recommended ease:** To be worn with approximately 1 to 5 inches (2.5 to 13 cm) of positive ease. Pick a size larger than your bust circumference. Sample shown is knit in size 3, worn with 2.75 inches (7 cm) of ease.

Materials

YARN
Worsted weight, De Rerum Natura Gilliatt (100% wool), 270 yds (250 m) per 100-g ball

YARDAGE/METERAGE
1109 (1183, 1246, 1343) (1463, 1550, 1651, 1761) (1923, 2021, 2127, 2238) yds /
1014 (1082, 1139, 1228) (1338, 1417, 1510, 1610) (1758, 1848, 1945, 2046) m

SHOWN IN
L'heure Bleue [4 (5, 5, 5) (6, 6, 6, 7) (7, 8, 8, 9) balls]

NEEDLES
For body and cowl: US 7 (4.5 mm), 24- to 32-inch (60- to 80-cm) circular needle
For sleeves: US 7 (4.5 mm), 12-inch (30-cm) circular needle or DPNs

NOTIONS
1 stitch marker
2 stitch holders
Tapestry needle
Waste yarn
Crochet hook

Gauge
19 sts × 26 rnds = 4 inches (10 cm) in stockinette stitch in the round (blocked)

Important note: Take time to check your gauge. This will ensure correct fit and yarn quantity.

(continued)

Special Techniques

Bobbles (page 152): For this pattern, I recommend doing 3 repetitions of (k1, yo) in the same stitch.

Crochet Provisional Cast-On (page 150)

German Short Rows: Follow these instructions to create German short rows.

Step 1: Start by working a right-side row, following the pattern until you are instructed to turn your work, and then turn work.

Step 2: On the wrong side, slip the stitch purlwise with yarn in front.

Step 3: Pull the yarn over the right needle, stretching the stitch so that two legs sit on the needle, and bring yarn in front to begin purling.

Step 4: Purl row as instructed and turn work when indicated.

Step 5: On the right side, bring yarn to front and slip the last stitch worked purlwise with yarn in front.

Step 6: Pull the yarn over the right needle, stretching the stitch so that two legs sit on the needle. Keep yarn in back to begin knitting.

Repeat steps 1–6 until all short rows have been worked.

On the next row, work the double stitches together as if they were only one stitch.

ABBREVIATIONS	
BO	bind off
BOR	beginning of round
CO	cast on
dec('d)	decrease(d)
inc'd	increased
k	knit
k2tog	knit two together
m	marker
m1l	make one left
mb	make bobble
p	purl
pm	place marker
rnd(s)	round(s)
RS	right side
sl	slip
ssk	slip slip knit
st(s)	stitch(es)
St st	stockinette stitch
tbl	through back loop
WS	wrong side
yo	yarn over

Amarelle Sweater Pattern

With waste yarn, CO 96 (96, 98, 100) (100, 104, 106, 112) (114, 114, 116, 118) sts using the Crochet Provisional Cast-On.

Pm to indicate BOR and join to work in the round.

Setup rnds 1–2: K all sts.

Setup rnd 3: [K 12 (6, 5, 4) (6, 5, 4, 4) (10, 7, 6, 5), m1l] to last 0 (0, 3, 0) (4, 4, 2, 0) (4, 2, 2, 3) sts, k to end. [104 (112, 117, 125) (116, 124, 132, 140) (125, 130, 135, 141) sts]

Setup rnd 4: K all sts, adding 0 (0, 3, 3) (3, 2, 1, 0) (1, 2, 3, 3) sts evenly distributed. [104 (112, 120, 128) (119, 126, 133, 140) (126, 132, 138, 144) sts]

BACK SHAPING

Back shaping is done using the German Short-Row Method (see instructions under the Special Techniques section of the pattern [page 86]).

Short row 1 (RS): K 26 (28, 30, 33) (30, 32, 35, 37) (33, 34, 37, 39), turn work.

Short row 2 (WS): P to 4 sts before m, turn work.

Short row 3: K 17 (19, 21, 24) (21, 23, 26, 28) (24, 25, 28, 30), turn work.

Short row 4: P to 8 sts before m, turn work.

SIZES 3–12 **ONLY**

Short row 5: K - (-, 13, 16) (13, 15, 18, 20) (16, 17, 20, 22), turn work.

Short row 6: P to 12 sts before m, turn work.

SIZES 8–12 **ONLY**

Short row 7: K - (-, -, -) (-, -, -, 12) (8, 9, 12, 14), turn work.

Short row 8: P to 16 sts before m, turn work.

ALL SIZES

Picking up rnd: K all sts, working the double sts together when you come to them.

Repeat picking up rnd one more time.

YOKE

Setup rnd (all sizes except size 2): Remove BOR m, k 7 (-, 3, 6) (9, 2, 6, 8) (1, 4, 8, 2), place BOR marker.

ALL SIZES

Work 54 (54, 54, 54) (63, 63, 63, 63) (73, 73, 73, 73) rows from chart number 1 (1, 1, 1) (2, 2, 2, 2) (3, 3, 3, 3), following the charts (pages 94–96) or the written instructions that follow. Then proceed to **End of Yoke** (page 91). [260 (280, 300, 320) (340, 360, 380, 400) (420, 440, 460, 480) sts]

[continued]

CHART 1 (SIZES 1–4)

Rnds 1–2: K all sts.

Rnd 3: (K4, mb, k3) around.

Rnd 4: K all sts.

Rnd 5: (K3, mb, p1, mb, k2) around.

Rnd 6: (K4, p1, k3) around.

Rnd 7: (Mb, k2, k tbl, p1, k tbl, k2) around.

Rnd 8: [K2, (p1, k tbl) twice, p1, k1] around.

Rnd 9: [P1, mb, yo, (p1, k tbl) twice, p1, yo, mb] around. [26 (28, 30, 32) sts inc'd]

Rnd 10: [P1, k2, (p1, k tbl) twice, p1, k2] around.

Rnd 11: [P1, k tbl, yo, (k tbl, p1) 3 times, k tbl, yo, k tbl] around. [26 (28, 30, 32) sts inc'd]

Rnds 12–13: (P1, k tbl) around.

Rnd 14: (P1, ssk, k tbl, p1, k tbl, yo, p1, yo, k tbl, p1, k tbl, k2tog) around.

Rnd 15: (P1, k1, k tbl, p1, k tbl, k1) around.

Rnd 16: (P1, ssk, p1, k tbl, yo, k1, p1, k1, yo, k tbl, p1, k2tog) around.

Rnd 17: (P1, k1, p1, k tbl, k2, p1, k2, k tbl, p1, k1) around.

Rnd 18: (P1, ssk, k tbl, yo, k2, p1, k2, yo, k tbl, k2tog) around.

Rnd 19: (P1, k1, k tbl, k3, p1, k3, k tbl, k1) around.

Rnd 20: (P1, ssk, yo, k3, p1, k3, yo, k2tog) around.

Rnd 21: (P1, k5) around.

Rnd 22: (P1, k1, yo, k4, p1, k4, yo, k1) around. [26 (28, 30, 32) sts inc'd]

Rnd 23: (P1, k6) around.

Rnd 24: (P1, k1, yo, k5, p1, k5, yo, k1) around. [26 (28, 30, 32) sts inc'd]

Rnd 25: (P1, k7) around.

Rnd 26: (P1, k1, yo, k4, k2tog, p1, ssk, k4, yo, k1) around.

Rnd 27: (P1, k2, yo, k3, k2tog, p1, ssk, k3, yo, k2) around.

Rnd 28: (P1, k3, yo, k2, k2tog, p1, ssk, k2, yo, k3) around.

Rnd 29: (P1, k1, mb, k2, yo, k1, k2tog, p1, ssk, k1, yo, k2, mb, k1) around.

Rnd 30: (P1, k5, yo, k2tog, p1, ssk, yo, k5) around.

Rnd 31: (P1, k3, mb, k3) around.

Rnd 32: Repeat rnd 25.

Rnd 33: (P1, k1, yo, k4, mb, k1, p1, k1, mb, k4, yo, k1) around. [26 (28, 30, 32) sts inc'd]

Rnd 34: (P1, k2, yo, ssk, k4, p1, k4, k2tog, yo, k2) around.

Rnd 35: (P1, k3, yo, ssk, k3, p1, k3, k2tog, yo, k3) around.

Rnd 36: (P1, k4, yo, ssk, k2, p1, k2, k2tog, yo, k4) around.

Rnd 37: (P1, k2, mb, k2, yo, ssk, k1, p1, k1, k2tog, yo, k2, mb, k2) around.

Rnd 38: (P1, k6, yo, ssk, p1, k2tog, yo, k6) around.

Rnd 39: (P1, k4, mb, k3, p1, k3, mb, k4) around.

Rnd 40: (P1, k1, yo, k7, p1, k7, yo, k1) around. [26 (28, 30, 32) sts inc'd]

Rnd 41: (P1, k2, yo, ssk, k3, mb, k1, p1, k1, mb, k3, k2tog, yo, k2) around.

Rnd 42: (P1, k3, yo, ssk, k4, p1, k4, k2tog, yo, k3) around.

Rnd 43: (P1, k1, mb, k2, yo, ssk, k3, p1, k3, k2tog, yo, k2, mb, k1) around.

Rnd 44: (P1, k5, yo, ssk, k2, p1, k2, k2tog, yo, k5) around.

Rnd 45: (P1, k3, mb, k2, yo, ssk, k1, p1, k1, k2tog, yo, k2, mb, k3) around.

Rnd 46: (P1, k7, yo, ssk, p1, k2tog, yo, k7) around.

Rnd 47: (K6, mb, k3, p1, k3, mb, k5) around.

Rnd 48: (K2, yo, ssk, k6, p1, k6, k2tog, yo, k1) around.

Rnd 49: (K3, yo, ssk, k3, mb, k1, p1, k1, mb, k3, k2tog, yo, k2) around.

Rnd 50: (K4, yo, ssk, k4, p1, k4, k2tog, yo, k3) around.

Rnd 51: (K5, yo, ssk, k3, p1, k3, k2tog, yo, k4) around.

Rnd 52: (K6, yo, ssk, k2, p1, k2, k2tog, yo, k5) around.

Rnd 53: (K7, yo, ssk, k1, p1, k1, k2tog, yo, k6) around.

Rnd 54: (K8, yo, ssk, p1, k2tog, yo, k7) around.

CHART 2 (SIZES 5–8)

Rnds 1–2: K all sts.

Rnd 3: (K3, mb, k3) around.

Rnd 4: K all sts.

Rnd 5: (K2, mb, p1, mb, k2) around.

Rnd 6: (K3, p1, k3) around.

Rnd 7: (Mb, k1, yo, k tbl, p1, k tbl, k2) around. [17 (18, 19, 20) sts inc'd]

Rnd 8: [K2, (p1, k tbl) twice, p1, k1] around.

Rnd 9: [P1, mb, yo, (p1, k tbl) twice, p1, yo, mb] around. [34 (36, 38, 40) sts inc'd]

Rnd 10: [P1, k2, (p1, k tbl) twice, p1, k2] around.

Rnd 11: [P1, k tbl, yo, (k tbl, p1) 3 times, k tbl, yo, k tbl] around. [34 (36, 38, 40) sts inc'd]

Rnds 12–14: (P1, k tbl) around.

Rnd 15: (P1, ssk, k tbl, p1, k tbl, yo, p1, yo, k tbl, p1, k tbl, k2tog) around.

Rnd 16: (P1, k1, k tbl, p1, k tbl, k1) around.

Rnd 17: (P1, ssk, p1, k tbl, yo, k1, p1, k1, yo, k tbl, p1, k2tog) around.

Rnd 18: (P1, k1, p1, k tbl, k2, p1, k2, k tbl, p1, k1) around.

Rnd 19: (P1, ssk, k tbl, yo, k2, p1, k2, yo, k tbl, k2tog) around.

Rnd 20: (P1, k1, k tbl, k3, p1, k3, k tbl, k1) around.

Rnd 21: (P1, ssk, yo, k3, p1, k3, yo, k2tog) around.

Rnd 22: (P1, k5) around.

Rnd 23: (P1, k1, yo, k4, p1, k4, yo, k1) around. [34 (36, 38, 40) sts inc'd]

Rnd 24: (P1, k6) around.

Rnd 25: (P1, k1, yo, k5, p1, k5, yo, k1) around. [34 (36, 38, 40) sts inc'd]

Rnd 26: (P1, k7) around.

Rnd 27: (P1, k1, yo, k4, k2tog, p1, ssk, k4, yo, k1) around.

Rnd 28: (P1, k2, yo, k3, k2tog, p1, ssk, k3, yo, k2) around.

Rnd 29: (P1, k3, yo, k2, k2tog, p1, ssk, k2, yo, k3) around.

Rnd 30: (P1, k1, mb, k2, yo, k1, k2tog, p1, ssk, k1, yo, k2, mb, k1) around.

Rnd 31: (P1, k5, yo, k2tog, p1, ssk, yo, k5) around.

Rnd 32: (P1, k3, mb, k3) around.

Rnd 33: Repeat rnd 26.

Rnd 34: (P1, k1, yo, k4, mb, k1, p1, k1, mb, k4, yo, k1) around. [34 (36, 38, 40) sts inc'd]

Rnd 35: (P1, k2, yo, ssk, k4, p1, k4, k2tog, yo, k2) around.

Rnd 36: (P1, k3, yo, ssk, k3, p1, k3, k2tog, yo, k3) around.

Rnd 37: (P1, k4, yo, ssk, k2, p1, k2, k2tog, yo, k4) around.

Rnd 38: (P1, k2, mb, k2, yo, ssk, k1, p1, k1, k2tog, yo, k2, mb, k2) around.

Rnd 39: (P1, k6, yo, ssk, p1, k2tog, yo, k6) around.

Rnd 40: (P1, k4, mb, k3, p1, k3, mb, k4) around.

Rnd 41: (P1, k1, yo, k7, p1, k7, yo, k1) around. [34 (36, 38, 40) sts inc'd]

Rnd 42: (P1, k2, yo, ssk, k3, mb, k1, p1, k1, mb, k3, k2tog, yo, k2) around.

Rnd 43: (P1, k3, yo, ssk, k4, p1, k4, k2tog, yo, k3) around.

Rnd 44: (P1, k1, mb, k2, yo, ssk, k3, p1, k3, k2tog, yo, k2, mb, k1) around.

[continued]

Rnd 45: (P1, k5, yo, ssk, k2, p1, k2, k2tog, yo, k5) around.

Rnd 46: (P1, k3, mb, k2, yo, ssk, k1, p1, k1, k2tog, yo, k2, mb, k3) around.

Rnd 47: (P1, k7, yo, ssk, p1, k2tog, yo, k7) around.

Rnd 48: (P1, k5, mb, k3, p1, k3, mb, k5) around.

Rnd 49: (P1, k1, yo, ssk, k6, p1, k6, k2tog, yo, k1) around.

Rnds 50–55: Repeat rnds 42–47.

Rnd 56: (K6, mb, k3, p1, k3, mb, k5) around.

Rnd 57: (K2, yo, ssk, k6, p1, k6, k2tog, yo, k1) around.

Rnd 58: (K3, yo, ssk, k3, mb, k1, p1, k1, mb, k3, k2tog, yo, k2) around.

Rnd 59: (K4, yo, ssk, k4, p1, k4, k2tog, yo, k3) around.

Rnd 60: (K5, yo, ssk, k3, p1, k3, k2tog, yo, k4) around.

Rnd 61: (K6, yo, ssk, k2, p1, k2, k2tog, yo, k5) around.

Rnd 62: (K7, yo, ssk, k1, p1, k1, k2tog, yo, k6) around.

Rnd 63: (K8, yo, ssk, p1, k2tog, yo, k7) around.

CHART 3 (SIZES 9–12)

Rnds 1–2: K all sts.

Rnd 3: (K3, mb, k2) around.

Rnd 4: K all sts.

Rnd 5: (K2, mb, p1, mb, k1) around.

Rnd 6: (K3, p1, k2) around.

Rnd 7: (Mb, k1, yo, k tbl, p1, k tbl, yo, k1) around. [42 (44, 46, 48) sts inc'd]

Rnd 8: [K2, (p1, k tbl) twice, p1, k1] around.

Rnd 9: [P1, mb, yo, (p1, k tbl) twice, p1, yo, mb] around. [42 (44, 46, 48) sts inc'd]

Rnd 10: [P1, k2, (p1, k tbl) twice, p1, k2] around.

Rnd 11: [P1, k tbl, yo, (k tbl, p1) 3 times, k tbl, yo, k tbl] around. [42 (44, 46, 48) sts inc'd]

Rnds 12–16: (P1, k tbl) around.

Rnd 17: (P1, ssk, k tbl, p1, k tbl, yo, p1, yo, k tbl, p1, k tbl, k2tog) around.

Rnd 18: (P1, k1, k tbl, p1, k tbl, k1) around.

Rnd 19: (P1, ssk, p1, k tbl, yo, k1, p1, k1, yo, k tbl, p1, k2tog) around.

Rnd 20: (P1, k1, p1, k tbl, k2, p1, k2, k tbl, p1, k1) around.

Rnd 21: (P1, ssk, k tbl, yo, k2, p1, k2, yo, k tbl, k2tog) around.

Rnd 22: (P1, k1, k tbl, k3, p1, k3, k tbl, k1) around.

Rnd 23: (P1, ssk, yo, k3, p1, k3, yo, k2tog) around.

Rnd 24: (P1, k5) around.

Rnd 25: (P1, k1, yo, k4, p1, k4, yo, k1) around. [42 (44, 46, 48) sts inc'd]

Rnd 26: (P1, k6) around.

Rnd 27: (P1, k1, yo, k5, p1, k5, yo, k1) around. [42 (44, 46, 48) sts inc'd]

Rnd 28: (P1, k7) around.

Rnd 29: (P1, k1, yo, k4, k2tog, p1, ssk, k4, yo, k1) around.

Rnd 30: (P1, k2, yo, k3, k2tog, p1, ssk, k3, yo, k2) around.

Rnd 31: (P1, k3, yo, k2, k2tog, p1, ssk, k2, yo, k3) around.

Rnd 32: (P1, k1, mb, k2, yo, k1, k2tog, p1, ssk, k1, yo, k2, mb, k1) around.

Rnd 33: (P1, k5, yo, k2tog, p1, ssk, yo, k5) around.

Rnd 34: (P1, k3, mb, k3) around.

Rnd 35: Repeat rnd 28.

Rnd 36: (P1, k5, mb, k1, p1, k1, mb, k5) around.

Rnd 37: (P1, k1, yo, ssk, k4, p1, k4, k2tog, yo, k1) around.

Rnd 38: (P1, k2, yo, ssk, k3, p1, k3, k2tog, yo, k2) around.

Rnd 39: (P1, k3, yo, ssk, k2, p1, k2, k2tog, yo, k3) around.

Rnd 40: (P1, k1, mb, k2, yo, ssk, k1, p1, k1, k2tog, yo, k2, mb, k1) around.

Rnd 41: (P1, k5, yo, ssk, p1, k2tog, yo, k5) around.

Rnd 42: Repeat rnd 34.

Rnd 43: Repeat rnd 28.

Rnd 44: (P1, k1, yo, k4, mb, k1, p1, k1, mb, k4, yo, k1) around. [42 (44, 46, 48) sts inc'd]

Rnd 45: (P1, k2, yo, ssk, k4, p1, k4, k2tog, yo, k2) around.

Rnd 46: (P1, k3, yo, ssk, k3, p1, k3, k2tog, yo, k3) around.

Rnd 47: (P1, k4, yo, ssk, k2, p1, k2, k2tog, yo, k4) around.

Rnd 48: (P1, k2, mb, k2, yo, ssk, k1, p1, k1, k2tog, yo, k2, mb, k2) around.

Rnd 49: (P1, k6, yo, ssk, p1, k2tog, yo, k6) around.

Rnd 50: (P1, k4, mb, k3, p1, k3, mb, k4) around.

Rnd 51: (P1, k8) around.

Rnd 52: (P1, k1, yo, ssk, k3, mb, k1, p1, k1, mb, k3, k2tog, yo, k1) around.

Rnds 53–58: Repeat rnds 45–50.

Rnd 59: (P1, k1, yo, k7, p1, k7, yo, k1) around. [42 (44, 46, 48) sts inc'd]

Rnd 60: (P1, k2, yo, ssk, k3, mb, k1, p1, k1, mb, k3, k2tog, yo, k2) around.

Rnd 61: (P1, k3, yo, ssk, k4, p1, k4, k2tog, yo, k3) around.

Rnd 62: (P1, k1, mb, k2, yo, ssk, k3, p1, k3, k2tog, yo, k2, mb, k1) around.

Rnd 63: (P1, k5, yo, ssk, k2, p1, k2, k2tog, yo, k5) around.

Rnd 64: (P1, k3, mb, k2, yo, ssk, k1, p1, k1, k2tog, yo, k2, mb, k3) around.

Rnd 65: (P1, k7, yo, ssk, p1, k2tog, yo, k7) around.

Rnd 66: (K6, mb, k3, p1, k3, mb, k5) around.

Rnd 67: (K2, yo, ssk, k6, p1, k6, k2tog, yo, k1) around.

Rnd 68: (K3, yo, ssk, k3, mb, k1, p1, k1, mb, k3, k2tog, yo, k2) around.

Rnd 69: (K4, yo, ssk, k4, p1, k4, k2tog, yo, k3) around.

Rnd 70: (K5, yo, ssk, k3, p1, k3, k2tog, yo, k4) around.

Rnd 71: (K6, yo, ssk, k2, p1, k2, k2tog, yo, k5) around.

Rnd 72: (K7, yo, ssk, k1, p1, k1, k2tog, yo, k6) around.

Rnd 73: (K8, yo, ssk, p1, k2tog, yo, k7) around.

END OF YOKE

K all sts for 0 (1, 1, 5) (0, 0, 4, 6) (0, 2, 5, 7) rnds.

SEPARATE BODY AND SLEEVES

The following instructions will create two rnds.

Remove BOR m.

Back: K 67 (80, 83, 86) (89, 102, 106, 108) (121, 124, 128, 142) sts; CO 2 (2, 1, 1) (1, 1, 1, 2) (2, 2, 2, 2) sts;

Sleeve: Sl 56 (60, 64, 68) (72, 76, 78, 84) (88, 92, 94, 96) sts to holder;

Front: K 74 (80, 86, 92) (98, 104, 112, 116) (122, 128, 136, 144) sts;

Sleeve: Sl 56 (60, 64, 68) (72, 76, 78, 84) (88, 92, 94, 96) sts to holder;

Back: CO 2 (2, 1, 1) (1, 1, 1, 2) (2, 2, 2, 2) sts; pm to indicate BOR; k 7 (0, 3, 6) (9, 2, 6, 8) (1, 4, 8, 2) sts to live needles.

K to end of rnd.

[**Live st count at bust:** 152 (164, 174, 186) (198, 210, 226, 236) (248, 260, 276, 292) sts]

[continued]

BODY

Work in St st until sweater measures 12 (12.5, 12.5, 13) (13, 13.5, 13.5, 14) (14, 14.5, 14.5, 15) inches / 30.5 (32, 32, 33) (33, 34.5, 34.5, 35.5) (35.5, 37, 37, 38) cm from underarm or 2.5 inches (6.5 cm) less than the desired finished length.

Dec rnd: [K 7 (8, 7, 8) (9, 7, 8, 7) (8, 8, 7, 8), k2tog] to last 8 (4, 12, 6) (0, 12, 6, 20) (8, 20, 24, 12) sts, k to end. [136 (148, 156, 168) (180, 188, 204, 212) (224, 236, 248, 264) sts]

Work in (k2, p2) ribbing for 2.5 inches (6.5 cm).

BO all sts in pattern.

SLEEVES

Both sleeves are worked the same way.

Join yarn at right side of underarm.

Pick up and k 3 (2, 2, 1) (1, 1, 1, 2) (3, 3, 3, 3) sts from underarm, pm to indicate BOR; pick up and k 3 (2, 2, 1) (1, 1, 1, 2) (3, 3, 3, 3) more sts from underarm; k 56 (60, 64, 68) (72, 76, 78, 84) (88, 92, 94, 96) sts from holder; k to BOR m. [62 (64, 68, 70) (74, 78, 80, 88) (94, 98, 100, 102) sts]

K all sts for 10 (9, 7, 8) (7, 5, 6, 4) (4, 4, 4, 4) rnds.

Dec rnd: K1, k2tog, k to 3 before m, ssk, k1. [2 sts dec'd]

Work 1 dec rnd followed by 10 (9, 7, 8) (7, 5, 6, 4) (4, 4, 4, 4) rnds in St st (k all sts), 7 (8, 10, 9) (11, 13, 12, 16) (17, 19, 18, 19) times total.

[48 (48, 48, 52) (52, 52, 56, 56) (60, 60, 64, 64) sts]

K all sts until sleeve measures 15 (15, 15.25, 15.25) (15.5, 15.5, 15.75, 16) (16.25, 16.25, 16.5, 16.5) inches / 38 (38, 39, 39) (39.5, 39.5, 40, 40.5) (41.5, 41.5, 42, 42) cm from underarm, or 2 inches (5 cm) less than the desired finished length.

NEXT RND

Sizes 1–3: (K4, ssk) around. [8 sts dec'd]

Sizes 4–6: (K4, ssk) to last 4 sts, k4. [8 sts dec'd]

Sizes 7–8: (K5, ssk) around. [8 sts dec'd]

Sizes 9–10: (K5, ssk) to last 4 sts, k4. [8 sts dec'd]

Sizes 11–12: (K6, ssk) around. [8 sts dec'd]

[40 (40, 40, 44) (44, 44, 48, 48) (52, 52, 56, 56) sts]

ALL SIZES

Work in (k2, p2) ribbing for 2 inches (5 cm).

BO all sts in pattern.

COWL

Carefully undo the provisional CO and put 96 (96, 98, 100) (100, 104, 106, 112) (114, 114, 116, 118) sts back on needles.

Setup rnd: Work in (k3, p2) ribbing, working 1 (1, 3, 0) (0, 4, 1, 2) (4, 4, 1, 3) dec evenly distributed. [95 (95, 95, 100) (100, 100, 105, 110) (110, 110, 115, 115) sts]

Work in (k3, p2) ribbing for 1 inch (2.5 cm).

Dec rnd: (K1, k2tog, p2) around. [76 (76, 76, 80) (80, 80, 84, 88) (88, 88, 92, 92) sts]

Work in (k2, p2) ribbing for 5 inches (13 cm) or the desired finished length.

BO all sts in pattern.

For a shorter cowl, you can omit the dec rnd and second ribbing section, and BO after the first ribbing section is done.

FINISHING

Weave in all ends. Block to the desired dimensions.

CHART KEY

☐	knit
Ｏ	yo
•	purl
＼	ssk
／	k2tog
⓪	bobble
Ω	k tbl
☐	repeat
▓	no stitch

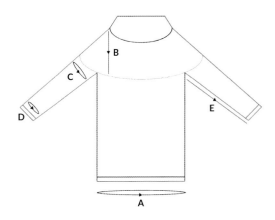

A: CIRCUMFERENCE AT BUST, WAIST AND HIPS

32 (34.5, 36.75, 39.25) (41.75, 44.25, 47.5, 49.75) (52.25, 54.75, 58, 61.5) inches

81.5 (87.5, 93.5, 99.5) (106, 112.5, 120.5, 126.5) (132.5, 139, 147.5, 156) cm

B: YOKE LENGTH

8.25 (8.5, 8.5, 9) (9.75, 9.75, 10.25, 10.5) (11.25, 11.5, 12, 12.25) inches

21 (21.5, 21.5, 23) (25, 25, 26, 26.5) (28.5, 29, 30.5, 31) cm

C: SLEEVE CIRCUMFERENCE AT TOP ARM

13 (13.5, 14.25, 14.75) (15.5, 16.5, 16.75, 18.5) (19.75, 20.75, 21, 21.5) inches

33 (34.5, 36, 37.5) (39.5, 42, 42.5, 47) (50, 52.5, 53.5, 54.5) cm

D: SLEEVE CIRCUMFERENCE AT WRIST

8.5 (8.5, 8.5, 9.25) (9.25, 9.25, 10, 10) (11, 11, 11.75, 11.75) inches

21.5 (21.5, 21.5, 23.5) (23.5, 23.5, 25.5, 25.5) (28, 28, 30, 30) cm

E: SLEEVE LENGTH AT UNDERARM

17 (17, 17.25, 17.25) (17.5, 17.5, 17.75, 18) (18.25, 18.25, 18.5, 18.5) inches

43 (43, 44, 44) (44.5, 44.5, 45, 45.5) (46.5, 46.5, 47, 47) cm

[continued]

CHART 1 (BOTTOM)

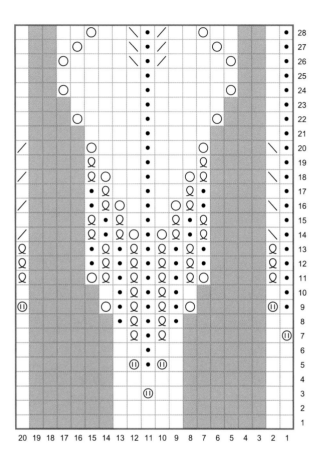

CHART 1 (TOP)

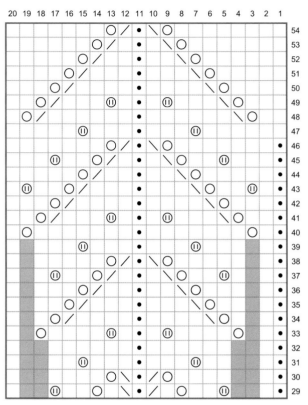

CHART 2 (BOTTOM)   CHART 2 (TOP)

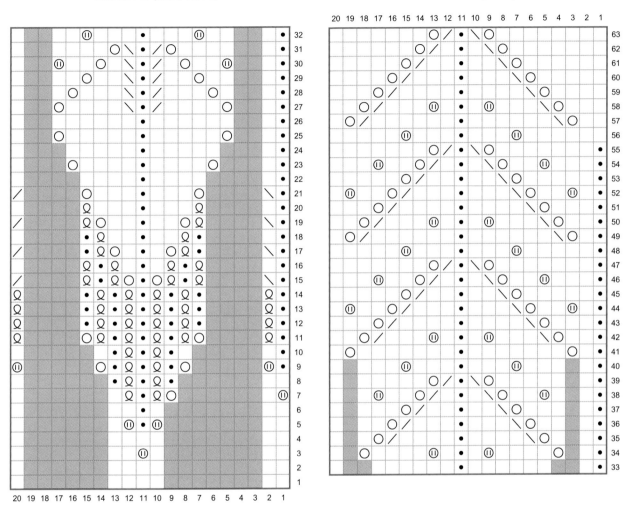

CHART 3 (BOTTOM) CHART 3 (TOP)

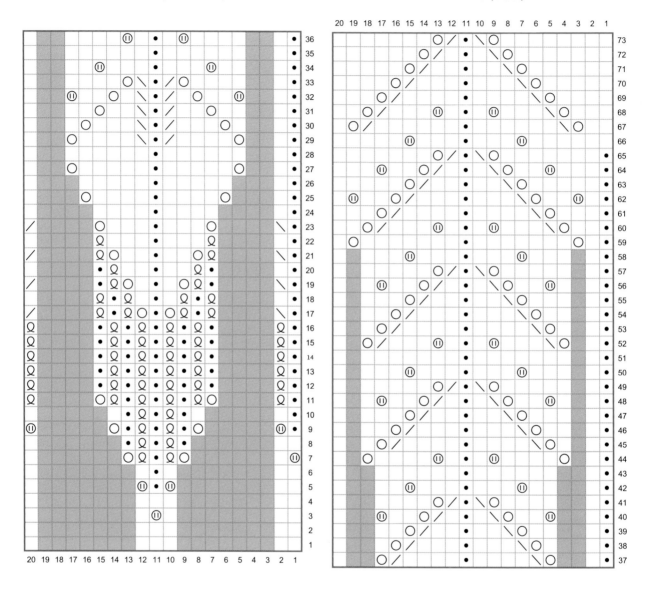

Pinnate Tank Top

Some people are admittedly sock knitters, while some prefer garments, hats or shawls. Even though I like all kinds of projects, knitted tank tops are possibly my favorite. They give me the satisfaction of having made a proper garment, yet they use low yardage and come together so quickly. While it may seem counterproductive to wear knitted garments during the warmer months, I've found that it's actually the opposite. When using cotton, linen, silk or even plied and treated wool, these garments flow in such a manner that they feel even lighter than most store-bought tops. In the colder months, they can be layered with a knitted cardigan or a pretty blazer, adding a dainty look to any outfit. I designed the Pinnate Tank Top to be romantic, flowy and lightweight. The lightness of the top is thanks to the lace pattern on the bottom. The lace part and the straps can be made longer or shorter as desired, and the top-down construction makes this top easy to customize.

Construction

This piece is worked from the top down, starting with the top parts of the back and the front, both worked flat in stockinette stitch. The pieces are joined together at the underarm, where working in the round begins. The bottom part starts with a section worked in stockinette stitch, followed by a lace pattern that gets larger by the bottom, to create a flattering A-line shape.

Skill Level: Intermediate

Sizes

- 1 (2, 3, 4) (5, 6, 7, 8) (9, 10, 11)

Finished Measurements

- Finished bust: 31.5 (34.5, 37.75, 40.75) (44, 47.25, 50.25, 53.5) (56.5, 59.75, 62.75) inches / 80 (87.5, 96, 103.5) (112, 120, 127.5, 136) (143.5, 152, 159.5) cm

- Recommended ease: Pick a size close to your bust circumference for a fitted tank, or 1–3 inches (2.5–8) cm larger for a looser fit. Sample shown is knit in size 2, worn with 2 inches (5 cm) of ease.

Materials

YARN
Light fingering weight, Emilia & Philomene Simone (70% organic wool; 30% linen), 510 yds (466 m) per 100-g skein

YARDAGE/METERAGE
648 (717, 811, 881) (964, 1058, 1140, 1203) (1309, 1382, 1466) yds /
593 (656, 742, 806) (881, 967, 1042, 1100) (1197, 1264, 1341) m

SHOWN IN
Camelia [2 (2, 2, 2) (2, 2, 3, 3) (3, 3, 3) skeins]

NEEDLES
For ribbing: US 0 (2 mm), 24- or 32-inch (60- or 80-cm) circular needles
For body: US 2 (2.75 mm), 24- or 32-inch (60- or 80-cm) circular needles
For straps: US 0 (2 mm), 3 DPNs

NOTIONS
5 stitch markers
Stitch holder
Tapestry needle

Gauge

28 sts × 34 rows = 4 inches (10 cm) in stockinette stitch, using larger needle (blocked)

27 sts × 34 rows = 4 inches (10 cm) in (k1, p1) ribbing, using smaller needle (blocked)

Important note: Take time to check your gauge. This will ensure correct fit and yarn quantity.

[continued]

ABBREVIATIONS	
BO	bind off
BOR	beginning of round
CO	cast on
inc('d)	increase(d)
k	knit
k2tog	knit two together
m	marker
m1r	make one right
m1l	make one left
p	purl
pfb	purl front and back
pm	place marker
rm	remove marker
rnd(s)	round(s)
RS	right side
sl	slip
sm	slip marker
ssk	slip slip knit
st(s)	stitch(es)
WS	wrong side
yo	yarn over

Pinnate Tank Top Pattern

BACK UPPER BODY

With smaller needles, CO 55 (59, 63, 67) (69, 73, 75, 77) (79, 83, 87) sts.

Starting and ending with a WS row, work in ribbing for 0.5 inch (1.5 cm), the following way:

Ribbing WS row: (P1, k1) to last st, p1.

Ribbing RS row: (K1, p1) to last st, k1.

Switch to larger needles.

Pm after the third st and before the last 3 sts.

STEP 1

Increase at each armhole edge, at every RS row, working both rows 14 (13, 12, 9) (9, 10, 8, 5) (3, 5, 2) times [28 (26, 24, 18) (18, 20, 16, 10) (6, 10, 4) rows total], the following way:

Step 1 RS row: K3, sm, m1l, k to last 3 sts, m1r, sm, k3. [2 sts inc'd]

Step 1 WS row: K3, sm, p to last 3 sts, sm, k3.

[83 (85, 87, 85) (87, 93, 91, 87) (85, 93, 91) sts]

STEP 2

Increase twice at each armhole edge, at every RS row, working both rows 5 (7, 9, 12) (14, 15, 18, 21) (24, 24, 27) times [10 (14, 18, 24) (28, 30, 36, 42) (48, 48, 54) rows total], the following way:

Step 2 RS row: K3, sm, m1l, k6, m1l, k to last 9 sts, m1r, k6, m1r, sm, k3. [4 sts inc'd]

Step 2 WS row: K3, sm, p to last 3 sts, sm, k3.

[103 (113, 123, 133) (143, 153, 163, 171) (181, 189, 199) sts]

Cut yarn and place sts on hold.

FRONT UPPER BODY

Work the front as for the back. When finished, leave the yarn attached and sts on the needles.

[continued]

JOINING BACK AND FRONT

With RS facing, place sts from the back on the live needles, after the front, so the next row starts at the first st of the front.

Joining round: Using the cable CO method, CO 3 (4, 4, 5) (5, 6, 6, 8) (8, 10, 10) sts, place additional m to indicate BOR, CO 4 (4, 5, 5) (6, 6, 7, 8) (9, 10, 11) sts, k those sts.

From second piece: K3, sm, k to next m, sm, k3.

CO 7 (8, 9, 10) (11, 12, 13, 16) (17, 20, 21) sts.

From first piece: K3, sm, k to last m, sm, k3.

[**Live sts at bust:** 220 (242, 264, 286) (308, 330, 352, 374) (396, 418, 440) sts]

Join to work in the round.

BODY

Note: You can work the straps before finishing the body. Knit them to the desired length and adjust the body length accordingly.

Body setup rnd 1: P 6 (6, 7, 7) (8, 8, 9, 10) (11, 12, 13), k1, sm, k to next m, sm, k1, p 11 (12, 13, 14) (15, 16, 17, 20) (21, 24, 25), k1, rm, k to next m, sm, k1, p 5 (6, 6, 7) (7, 8, 8, 10) (10, 12, 12).

Body setup rnd 2: K all sts.

Body setup rnd 3: P 5 (5, 6, 6) (7, 7, 8, 9) (10, 11, 12), k2, rm, k to next m, rm, k2, p 9 (10, 11, 12) (13, 14, 15, 18) (19, 22, 23), k to next m, rm, k2, p 4 (5, 5, 6) (6, 7, 7, 9) (9, 11, 11).

Body rnd: K all sts.

Work body rnd until top measures 7.5 (7.75, 8.5, 8.5) (9, 9.75, 10, 10) (10.75, 11, 11.25) inches / 19 (19.5, 21.5, 21.5) (23, 25, 25.5, 25.5) (27.5, 28, 28.5) cm from CO edge.

LACE SECTION

Work 84 rows, following the Lace Pattern Chart (page 103) or the written instructions that follow. Then proceed to **Bottom Ribbing** (page 102).

Note: To achieve a longer top, rows 74–84 can be repeated. To achieve a shorter top, rows 74–84 can be omitted. To create a more flowing effect, you can use a larger needle size on the lace part.

WRITTEN INSTRUCTIONS

Rnd 1: (P1, k9, yo, p3, yo, k9) around. [20 (22, 24, 26) (28, 30, 32, 34) (36, 38, 40) sts inc'd; 240 (264, 288, 312) (336, 360, 384, 408) (432, 458, 480) sts]

Rnd 2: (P1, k6, k2tog, k1, yo, k1, p3, k1, yo, k1, ssk, k6) around.

Rnd 3: (P1, k5, k2tog, k1, yo, k2, p3, k2, yo, k1, ssk, k5) around.

Rnd 4: (P1, k4, k2tog, k1, yo, k3, p3, k3, yo, k1, ssk, k4) around.

Rnd 5: (P1, k3, k2tog, k1, yo, k4, p3, k4, yo, k1, ssk, k3) around.

Rnd 6: (P1, k2, k2tog, k1, yo, k5, p3, k5, yo, k1, ssk, k2) around.

Rnd 7: (P1, k1, k2tog, k1, yo, k6, p3, k6, yo, k1, ssk, k1) around.

Rnd 8: (P1, k2tog, k1, yo, k7, p3, k7, yo, k1, ssk) around.

Rnd 9: (P1, k7, k2tog, k1, yo, p3, yo, k1, ssk, k7) around.

Rnds 10–17: Repeat rnds 2–9.

Rnds 18–24: Repeat rnds 2–8.

Rnd 25: (P1, k10, yo, p3, yo, k10) around. [20 (22, 24, 26) (28, 30, 32, 34) (36, 38, 40) sts inc'd; 260 (286, 312, 338) (364, 390, 416, 442) (468, 494, 520) sts]

Rnd 26: (P1, k7, k2tog, k1, yo, k1, p3, k1, yo, k1, ssk, k7) around.

Rnd 27: (P1, k6, k2tog, k1, yo, k2, p3, k2, yo, k1, ssk, k6) around.

Rnd 28: (P1, k5, k2tog, k1, yo, k3, p3, k3, yo, k1, ssk, k5) around.

Rnd 29: (P1, k4, k2tog, k1, yo, k4, p3, k4, yo, k1, ssk, k4) around.

Rnd 30: (P1, k3, k2tog, k1, yo, k5, p3, k5, yo, k1, ssk, k3) around.

Rnd 31: (P1, k2, k2tog, k1, yo, k6, p3, k6, yo, k1, ssk, k2) around.

Rnd 32: (P1, k1, k2tog, k1, yo, k7, p3, k7, yo, k1, ssk, k1) around.

Rnd 33: (P1, k2tog, k1, yo, k8, p3, k8, yo, k1, ssk) around.

Rnd 34: (P1, k8, k2tog, k1, yo, p3, yo, k1, ssk, k8) around.

Rnds 35–42: Repeat rnds 26–33.

Rnd 43: (P1, k11, yo, p3, yo, k11) around. [20 (22, 24, 26) (28, 30, 32, 34) (36, 38, 40) sts inc'd; 280 (308, 336, 364) (392, 420, 448, 476) (504, 532, 560) sts]

Rnd 44: (P1, k8, k2tog, k1, yo, k1, p3, k1, yo, k1, ssk, k8) around.

Rnd 45: (P1, k7, k2tog, k1, yo, k2, p3, k2, yo, k1, ssk, k7) around.

Rnd 46: (P1, k6, k2tog, k1, yo, k3, p3, k3, yo, k1, ssk, k6) around.

Rnd 47: (P1, k5, k2tog, k1, yo, k4, p3, k4, yo, k1, ssk, k5) around.

Rnd 48: (P1, k4, k2tog, k1, yo, k5, p3, k5, yo, k1, ssk, k4) around.

Rnd 49: (P1, k3, k2tog, k1, yo, k6, p3, k6, yo, k1, ssk, k3) around.

Rnd 50: (P1, k2, k2tog, k1, yo, k7, p3, k7, yo, k1, ssk, k2) around.

Rnd 51: (P1, k1, k2tog, k1, yo, k8, p3, k8, yo, k1, ssk, k1) around.

Rnd 52: (P1, k2tog, k1, yo, k9, p3, k9, yo, k1, ssk) around.

Rnd 53: (P1, k9, k2tog, k1, yo, p3, yo, k1, ssk, k9) around.

Rnds 54–62: Repeat rnds 44–52.

Rnd 63: (P1, k12, yo, p3, yo, k12) around. [20 (22, 24, 26) (28, 30, 32, 34) (36, 38, 40) sts inc'd; 300 (330, 360, 390) (420, 450, 480, 510) (540, 570, 600) sts]

Rnd 64: (P1, k9, k2tog, k1, yo, k1, p3, k1, yo, k1, ssk, k9) around.

Rnd 65: (P1, k8, k2tog, k1, yo, k2, p3, k2, yo, k1, ssk, k8) around.

Rnd 66: (P1, k7, k2tog, k1, yo, k3, p3, k3, yo, k1, ssk, k7) around.

Rnd 67: (P1, k6, k2tog, k1, yo, k4, p3, k4, yo, k1, ssk, k6) around.

Rnd 68: (P1, k5, k2tog, k1, yo, k5, p3, k5, yo, k1, ssk, k5) around.

Rnd 69: (P1, k4, k2tog, k1, yo, k6, p3, k6, yo, k1, ssk, k4) around.

Rnd 70: (P1, k3, k2tog, k1, yo, k7, p3, k7, yo, k1, ssk, k3) around.

Rnd 71: (P1, k2, k2tog, k1, yo, k8, p3, k8, yo, k1, ssk, k2) around.

[continued]

Rnd 72: (P1, k1, k2tog, k1, yo, k9, p3, k9, yo, k1, ssk, k1) around.

Rnd 73: (P1, k2tog, k1, yo, k10, p3, k10, yo, k1, ssk) around.

Rnd 74: (P1, k10, k2tog, k1, yo, p3, yo, k1, ssk, k10) around.

Rnds 75–84: Repeat rnds 64–73.

BOTTOM RIBBING

Switch to smaller needles.

Work in (p1, k1) ribbing until ribbing measures 1 inch (2.5 cm).

BO all sts in pattern.

STRAPS

On the front, with a DPN, pick up and k 6 sts from CO edge, starting at the first st at the left side.

Setup Row: Pfb all sts. [12 sts]

Turn work so RS is facing you. Separate sts on two DPNs, the following way:

(Sl 1 st to DPN placed in the back, sl 1 st to DPN placed in the front); repeat until all sts have been moved to the two DPNs.

Start working in the round, working from the front DPN first and then the back DPN.

K all sts until strap measures 6.5 (7.5, 8, 8) (8.5, 8.5, 9, 9.5) (10, 10.5, 11) inches / 16.5 (19, 20.5, 20.5) (21.5, 21.5, 23, 24) (25.5, 26.5, 28) cm.

BO all sts, using the three-needle BO method.

Turn work. Sew strap on the CO edge of the back of the top.

Repeat on the other side, picking up the last 6 sts on the right side.

FINISHING

Weave in all ends. Block to the desired dimensions.

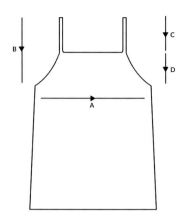

A: CIRCUMFERENCE AT BUST

31.5 (34.5, 37.75, 40.75) (44, 47.25, 50.25, 53.5) (56.5, 59.75, 62.75) inches

80 (87.5, 96, 103.5) (112, 120, 127.5, 136) (143.5, 152, 159.5) cm

B: TOTAL ARMHOLE DEPTH

7.75 (8.5, 9, 9) (9.75, 10.25, 10.5, 10.75) (11.25, 12, 12.25) inches

19.5 (21.5, 23, 23) (25, 26, 26.5, 27.5) (28.5, 30.5, 31) cm

C: STRAP LENGTH

3.25 (3.75, 4, 4) (4.25, 4.25, 4.5, 4.75) (5, 5.25, 5.5) inches

8.5 (9.5, 10, 10) (11, 11, 11.5, 12) (12.5, 13.5, 14) cm

D: ARMHOLE DEPTH (EXCLUDING STRAPS)

5 (5.25, 5.5, 5.5) (6, 6.25, 6.5, 6.5) (6.75, 7.25, 7.25) inches

12.5 (13.5, 14, 14) (15, 16, 16.5, 16.5) (17, 18.5, 18.5) cm

LACE PATTERN CHART (BOTTOM)

LACE PATTERN CHART (TOP)

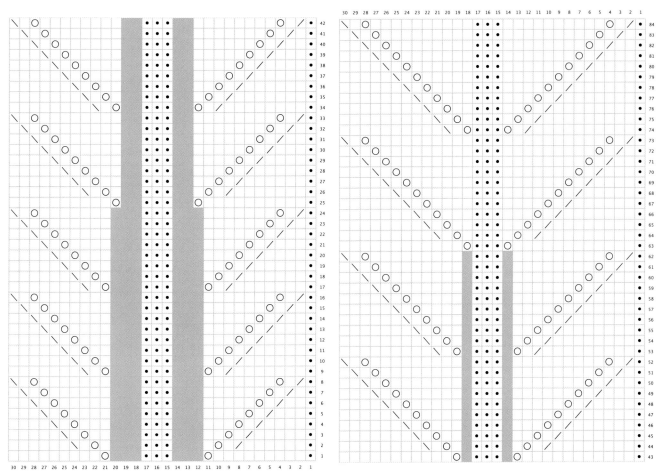

CHART KEY

□	knit
•	purl
O	yo
\	ssk
/	k2tog
▓	no stitch

Periiwinkle Shawl

Periwinkles are charming little flowers that spread rapidly and are often used as ground cover in gardens. They inspired me to design this shawl using a special stitch that creates little flowers, which cover most of the shawl. On the border, an open, leafy pattern balances this piece in a delicate way.

Construction

This shawl is worked sideways, with flowers aligned at regular intervals on most of the shawl. The design then transitions to a leafy pattern that creates an openwork border. A few rows of ribbing and a picot binding end the shawl. This project is adaptable in size: You can knit the flower section and the border longer or shorter to create a shawl that suits your preference (though your yardage will vary).

Skill Level: Intermediate

Size

- One size for adults

Finished Measurements

- 50 inches (127 cm) at top edge
- 45 inches (114.5 cm) at bottom edge
- 27.5 inches (70 cm) at border edge

Materials

YARN
Fingering weight, Julie Asselin Fino (75% merino; 15% cashmere; 10% silk), 400 yds (370 m) per 115-g skein

YARDAGE/METERAGE
640 yds (585 m)

SHOWN IN
Lamb's Ear (2 skeins)

Any fingering to DK weight yarn can be used for this pattern. Gauge, yardage and final size will vary.

NEEDLES
US 2 (2.75 mm), 32-inch (80-cm) circular needle, or size needed to obtain gauge

Important note: Gauge can vary according to your yarn and needle size. If your gauge differs, your shawl will have different dimensions from the prototype. Adjust the needle size to create a pleasing fabric. Make sure to plan for more yardage if you use a different yarn or wish to achieve a larger size.

NOTIONS
Tapestry needle

Gauge
28 sts × 34 rows = 4 inches (10 cm) in Body pattern (blocked)
27 sts × 36 rows = 4 inches (10 cm) in Border pattern (blocked)

[continued]

ABBREVIATIONS	
BO	bind off
CO	cast on
dec'd	decreased
inc'd	increased
k	knit
k2tog	knit two together
m1l	make one left
m1r	make one right
p	purl
p2tog	purl two together
p3tog	purl three together
RS	right side
ssk	slip slip knit
ssp	slip slip purl
st(s)	stitch(es)
tbl	through back loop
WS	wrong side
yo	yarn over

Periwinkle Shawl Pattern

You may work this shawl either from the charts or from the written instructions. Look for the separate sections as you proceed through the pattern.

- -

Note: The flower stitch pattern is worked in both the Setup and Body sections. It is worked over 4 rows. The number of stitches vary in this special stitch: It is worked over 3 stitches, it increases 4 stitches in row 1, decreases 2 stitches in row 3 and decreases 2 stitches in row 4. These increases and decreases are not shown in the stitch counts, as they do not affect the ultimate stitch count of the shawl.

When working from the charts, follow the Flower Stitch Chart (page 110) when the Setup Chart and Body Chart indicate to work a flower (over 3 stitches and 4 rows). The flower stitch pattern is integrated in the written instructions.

- -

SETUP

CO 3 sts.

Work from the Setup Chart (page 112) or the written instructions that follow over 46 rows. Then proceed to **Body** (page 108). [29 sts]

WRITTEN INSTRUCTIONS

Row 1 (RS): K all sts.

Row 2 (WS): K all sts.

Row 3: K1, m1r, k1, m1l, k1. [5 sts]

Row 4: K all sts.

Row 5: K2, m1r, k1, m1l, k2. [7 sts]

Row 6: K all sts.

Row 7: K3, m1r, k1, m1l, k3. [9 sts]

Row 8: K all sts.

Row 9: K3, p1, m1r, p1, m1l, p1, k3. [11 sts]

Row 10: K4, p1 tbl, k1, p1 tbl, k4.

Row 11: K3, p1, k1 tbl, m1r, p1, k1 tbl, p1, k3. [12 sts]

Row 12: K4, p1 tbl, k2, p1 tbl, k4.

Row 13: K3, p1, k1 tbl, p1, m1r, p1, k1 tbl, p1, k3. [13 sts]

Row 14: K4, p1 tbl, k1, p1, k1, p1 tbl, k4.

Row 15: K3, p1, k1 tbl, p1, k1, m1r, p1, k1 tbl, p1, k3. [14 sts]

Row 16: K4, p1 tbl, k1, p2, k1, p1 tbl, k4.

Row 17: K3, p1, k1 tbl, p1, k2, m1r, p1, k1 tbl, p1, k3. [15 sts]

Row 18: K4, p1 tbl, k1, p3, k1, p1 tbl, k4.

Row 19: K3, p1, k1 tbl, p1, k3, m1r, p1, k1 tbl, p1, k3. [16 sts]

Row 20: K4, p1 tbl, k1, p4, k1, p1 tbl, k4.

Row 21: K3, p1, k1 tbl, p1, k4, m1r, p1, k1 tbl, p1, k3. [17 sts]

Row 22: K4, p1 tbl, k1, p5, k1, p1 tbl, k4.

Row 23: K3, p1, k1 tbl, p1, k5, m1r, p1, k1 tbl, p1, k3. [18 sts]

Row 24: K4, p1 tbl, k1, p6, k1, p1 tbl, k4.

Row 25: K3, p1, k1 tbl, p1, k6, m1r, p1, k1 tbl, p1, k3. [19 sts]

Row 26: K4, p1 tbl, k1, p7, k1, p1 tbl, k4.

Row 27: K3, p1, k1 tbl, p1, k7, m1r, p1, k1 tbl, p1, k3. [20 sts]

Row 28: K4, p1 tbl, k2, p7, k1, p1 tbl, k4.

Row 29: K3, p1, k1 tbl, p1, k7, p1, m1r, p1, k1 tbl, p1, k3. [21 sts]

Row 30: K4, (p1 tbl, k1) twice, p7, k1, p1 tbl, k4.

Row 31: K3, p1, k1 tbl, p1, k7, p1, k1 tbl, m1r, p1, k1 tbl, p1, k3. [22 sts]

Row 32: K4, p1 tbl, k2, p1 tbl, k1, p7, k1, p1 tbl, k4.

Row 33: K3, p1, k1 tbl, p1, k7, p1, k1 tbl, p1, m1r, p1, k1 tbl, p1, k3. [23 sts]

Row 34: K4, p1 tbl, k1, p1, k1, p1 tbl, k1, p7, k1, p1 tbl, k4.

Row 35: K3, p1, k1 tbl, p1, k7, p1, k1 tbl, p1, k1, m1r, p1, k1 tbl, p1, k3. [24 sts]

Row 36: K4, p1 tbl, k1, p2, k1, p1 tbl, k1, p7, k1, p1 tbl, k4.

Row 37: K3, p1, k1 tbl, p1, k7, (yo, k1) 3 times, yo, k2, m1r, p1, k1 tbl, p1, k3. [25 sts]

Row 38: K4, p1 tbl, k1, p3, (k1, p1) 3 times, k1, p7, k1, p1 tbl, k4.

Row 39: K3, p1, k1 tbl, p1, k7, p1, ssk, k1, k2tog, p1, k3, m1r, p1, k1 tbl, p1, k3. [26 sts]

Row 40: K4, p1 tbl, k1, p4, k1, p3tog, k1, p7, k1, p1 tbl, k4. [26 sts]

Row 41: P1, k2, p1, k1 tbl, p1, k7, p1, k1 tbl, p1, k4, m1r, p1, k1 tbl, p1, k3. [27 sts]

Row 42: K4, p1 tbl, k1, p5, k1, p1 tbl, k1, p7, k1, p1 tbl, k4.

Row 43: K3, p1, k1 tbl, p1, k7, p1, k1 tbl, p1, k5, m1r, p1, k1 tbl, p1, k3. [28 sts]

Row 44: K4, p1 tbl, k1, p6, k1, p1 tbl, k1, p7, k1, p1 tbl, k4.

Row 45: K3, p1, k1 tbl, p1, k7, p1, k1 tbl, p1, k6, m1r, p1, k1 tbl, p1, k3. [29 sts]

Row 46: K4, (p1 tbl, k1, p7, k1) twice, p1 tbl, k4.

[continued]

BODY

Work from the Body Chart (page 111) or the written instructions that follow, working rows 1–20, 14 times, or any multiple of 2 times. [169 sts or any multiple of 10 + 29 sts]

Work rows 1–4 once more. [171 sts or any multiple of 10 + 31 sts]

Then proceed to **Border**.

WRITTEN INSTRUCTIONS

Row 1 (RS): K3, p1, k1 tbl, p1, [k7, (yo, k1) 3 times, yo] to last 13 sts, k7, m1r, p1, k1 tbl, p1, k3. [1 st inc'd]

Row 2 (WS): K4, p1 tbl, k2, p7, [(k1, p1) 3 times, k1, p7] to last 6 sts, k1, p1 tbl, k4.

Row 3: K3, p1, k1 tbl, p1, (k7, p1, ssk, k1, k2tog, p1) to last 14 sts, k7, p1, m1r, p1, k1 tbl, p1, k3. [1 st inc'd]

Row 4: K4, (p1 tbl, k1) twice, p7, (k1, p3tog, k1, p7) to last 6 sts, k1, p1 tbl, k4.

Row 5: K3, p1, k1 tbl, p1, (k7, p1, k1 tbl, p1) to last 15 sts, k7, p1, k1 tbl, m1r, p1, k1 tbl, p1, k3. [1 st inc'd]

Row 6: K4, p1 tbl, k2, p1 tbl, k1, p7, (k1, p1 tbl, k1, p7) to last 6 sts, k1, p1 tbl, k4.

Row 7: K3, p1, k1 tbl, p1, (k7, p1, k1 tbl, p1) to last 6 sts, m1r, p1, k1 tbl, p1, k3. [1 st inc'd]

Row 8: K4, p1 tbl, k1, p1, (k1, p1 tbl, k1, p7) to last 6 sts, k1, p1 tbl, k4.

Row 9: K3, p1, k1 tbl, p1, (k7, p1, k1 tbl, p1) to last 7 sts, k1, m1r, p1, k1 tbl, p1, k3. [1 st inc'd]

Row 10: K4, p1 tbl, k1, p2, (k1, p1 tbl, k1, p7) to last 6 sts, k1, p1 tbl, k4.

Row 11: K3, p1, k1 tbl, p1, [k7, (yo, k1) 3 times, yo] to last 8 sts, k2, m1r, p1, k1 tbl, p1, k3. [1 st inc'd]

Row 12: K4, p1 tbl, k1, p3, [(k1, p1) 3 times, k1, p7] to last 6 sts, k1, p1 tbl, k4.

Row 13: K3, p1, k1 tbl, p1, (k7, p1, ssk, k1, k2tog, p1) to last 9 sts, k3, m1r, p1, k1 tbl, p1, k3. [1 st inc'd]

Row 14: K4, p1 tbl, k1, p4, (k1, p3tog, k1, p7) to last 6 sts, k1, p1 tbl, k4. [2 sts dec'd in each pattern]

Row 15: K3, p1, k1 tbl, p1, (k7, p1, k1 tbl, p1) to last 10 sts, k4, m1r, p1, k1 tbl, p1, k3. [1 st inc'd]

Row 16: K4, p1 tbl, k1, p5, (k1, p1 tbl, k1, p7) to last 6 sts, k1, p1 tbl, k4.

Row 17: K3, p1, k1 tbl, p1, (k7, p1, k1 tbl, p1) to last 11 sts, k5, m1r, p1, k1 tbl, p1, k3. [1 st inc'd]

Row 18: K4, p1 tbl, k1, p6, (k1, p1 tbl, k1, p7) to last 6 sts, k1, p1 tbl, k4.

Row 19: K3, p1, k1 tbl, p1, (k7, p1, k1 tbl, p1) to last 12 sts, k6, m1r, p1, k1 tbl, p1, k3. [1 st inc'd]

Row 20: K4, p1 tbl, k1, p7, (k1, p1 tbl, k1, p7) to last 6 sts, k1, p1 tbl, k4.

BORDER

Work from the Border Chart (page 113) or the written instructions that follow, working rows 1–40 as many times as desired, ending at row 4, 8, 12, 16, 20, 24, 28, 32 or 40.

The prototype's border has 48 rows total. [195 sts]

Then proceed to **Final Border** (page 110).

WRITTEN INSTRUCTIONS

Row 1 (RS): K3, p1, (k1 tbl, p1, yo, k3, ssk, k3, k1 tbl, k3, k2tog, k3, yo, p1) to last 7 sts, k1 tbl, m1r, p1, k1 tbl, p1, k3. [1 st inc'd]

Row 2 (WS): K4, p1 tbl, k2, p1 tbl, (k1, p1, yo, p3, p2tog, p2, p1 tbl, p2, ssp, p3, yo, p1, k1, p1 tbl) to last 4 sts, k4.

Row 3: K3, p1, (k1 tbl, p1, k2, yo, k3, ssk, k1, k1 tbl, k1, k2tog, k3, yo, k2, p1) to last 8 sts, k1 tbl, p1, m1r, p1, k1 tbl, p1, k3. [1 st inc'd]

Row 4: K4, p1 tbl, k1, p1, k1, p1 tbl, (k1, p3, yo, p3, p2tog, p1 tbl, ssp, p3, yo, p3, k1, p1 tbl) to last 4 sts, k4.

Row 5: K3, p1, (k1 tbl, p1, yo, k3, ssk, k3, k1 tbl, k3, k2tog, k3, yo, p1) to last 9 sts, k1 tbl, p1, k1, m1r, p1, k1 tbl, p1, k3. [1 st inc'd]

Row 6: K4, p1 tbl, k1, p2, k1, p1 tbl, (k1, p1, yo, p3, p2tog, p2, p1 tbl, p2, ssp, p3, yo, p1, k1, p1 tbl) to last 4 sts, k4.

Row 7: K3, p1, (k1 tbl, p1, k2, yo, k3, ssk, k1, k1 tbl, k1, k2tog, k3, yo, k2, p1) to last 10 sts, k1 tbl, p1, k2, m1r, p1, k1 tbl, p1, k3. [1 st inc'd]

Row 8: K4, p1 tbl, k1, p3, k1, p1 tbl, (k1, p3, yo, p3, p2tog, p1 tbl, ssp, p3, yo, p3, k1, p1 tbl) to last 4 sts, k4.

Row 9: K3, p1, (k1 tbl, p1, yo, k3, ssk, k3, k1 tbl, k3, k2tog, k3, yo, p1) to last 11 sts, k1 tbl, p1, k3, m1r, p1, k1 tbl, p1, k3. [1 st inc'd]

Row 10: K4, p1 tbl, k1, p4, k1, p1 tbl, (k1, p1, yo, p3, p2tog, p2, p1 tbl, p2, ssp, p3, yo, p1, k1, p1 tbl) to last 4 sts, k4.

Row 11: K3, p1, (k1 tbl, p1, k2, yo, k3, ssk, k1, k1 tbl, k1, k2tog, k3, yo, k2, p1) to last 12 sts, k1 tbl, p1, k4, m1r, p1, k1 tbl, p1, k3. [1 st inc'd]

Row 12: K4, p1 tbl, k1, p5, k1, p1 tbl, (k1, p3, yo, p3, p2tog, p1 tbl, ssp, p3, yo, p3, k1, p1 tbl) to last 4 sts, k4.

Row 13: K3, p1, (k1 tbl, p1, yo, k3, ssk, k3, k1 tbl, k3, k2tog, k3, yo, p1) to last 13 sts, k1 tbl, p1, k5, m1r, p1, k1 tbl, p1, k3. [1 st inc'd]

Row 14: K4, p1 tbl, k1, p6, k1, p1 tbl, (k1, p1, yo, p3, p2tog, p2, p1 tbl, p2, ssp, p3, yo, p1, k1, p1 tbl) to last 4 sts, k4.

Row 15: K3, p1, (k1 tbl, p1, k2, yo, k3, ssk, k1, k1 tbl, k1, k2tog, k3, yo, k2, p1) to last 14 sts, k1 tbl, p1, k6, m1r, p1, k1 tbl, p1, k3. [1 st inc'd]

Row 16: K4, p1 tbl, k1, p7, k1, p1 tbl, (k1, p3, yo, p3, p2tog, p1 tbl, ssp, p3, yo, p3, k1, p1 tbl) to last 4 sts, k4.

Row 17: K3, p1, (k1 tbl, p1, yo, k3, ssk, k3, k1 tbl, k3, k2tog, k3, yo, p1) to last 15 sts, k1 tbl, p1, yo, k3, ssk, k2, m1r, p1, k1 tbl, p1, k3. [1 st inc'd]

Row 18: K4, p1 tbl, k1, p2, ssp, p3, yo, p1, k1, p1 tbl, (k1, p1, yo, p3, p2tog, p2, p1 tbl, p2, ssp, p3, yo, p1, k1, p1 tbl) to last 4 sts, k4.

Row 19: K3, p1, (k1 tbl, p1, k2, yo, k3, ssk, k1, k1 tbl, k1, k2tog, k3, yo, k2, p1) to last 16 sts, k1 tbl, p1, k2, yo, k3, ssk, k1, m1r, p1, k1 tbl, p1, k3. [1 st inc'd]

Row 20: K4, p1 tbl, k1, p1 tbl, ssp, p3, yo, p3, k1, p1 tbl, (k1, p3, yo, p3, p2tog, p1 tbl, ssp, p3, yo, p3, k1, p1 tbl) to last 4 sts, k4.

Row 21: K3, p1, (k1 tbl, p1, yo, k3, ssk, k3, k1 tbl, k3, k2tog, k3, yo, p1) to last 17 sts, k1 tbl, p1, yo, k3, ssk, k3, k1 tbl, m1r, p1, k1 tbl, p1, k3. [1 st inc'd]

Row 22: K4, p1 tbl, k1, p1, p1 tbl, p2, ssp, p3, yo, p1, k1, p1 tbl, (k1, p1, yo, p3, p2tog, p2, p1 tbl, p2, ssp, p3, yo, p1, k1, p1 tbl) to last 4 sts, k4.

Row 23: K3, p1, (k1 tbl, p1, k2, yo, k3, ssk, k1, k1 tbl, k1, k2tog, k3, yo, k2, p1) to last 18 sts, k1 tbl, p1, k2, yo, k3, ssk, k1, k1 tbl, k1, m1r, p1, k1 tbl, p1, k3. [1 st inc'd]

Row 24: K4, p1 tbl, k1, p2, p1 tbl, ssp, p3, yo, p3, k1, p1 tbl, (k1, p3, yo, p3, p2tog, p1 tbl, ssp, p3, yo, p3, k1, p1 tbl) to last 4 sts, k4.

Row 25: K3, p1, (k1 tbl, p1, yo, k3, ssk, k3, k1 tbl, k3, k2tog, k3, yo, p1) to last 19 sts, k1 tbl, p1, yo, k3, ssk, k3, k1 tbl, k2, m1r, p1, k1 tbl, p1, k3. [1 st inc'd]

Row 26: K4, p1 tbl, k1, p3, p1 tbl, p2, ssp, p3, yo, p1, k1, p1 tbl, (k1, p1, yo, p3, p2tog, p2, p1 tbl, p2, ssp, p3, yo, p1, k1, p1 tbl) to last 4 sts, k4.

Row 27: K3, p1, (k1 tbl, p1, k2, yo, k3, ssk, k1, k1 tbl, k1, k2tog, k3, yo, k2, p1) to last 20 sts, k1 tbl, p1, k2, yo, k3, ssk, k1, k1 tbl, k3, m1r, p1, k1 tbl, p1, k3. [1 st inc'd]

Row 28: K4, p1 tbl, k1, p4, p1 tbl, ssp, p3, yo, p3, k1, p1 tbl, (k1, p3, yo, p3, p2tog, p1 tbl, ssp, p3, yo, p3, k1, p1 tbl) to last 4 sts, k4.

[continued]

Row 29: K3, p1, (k1 tbl, p1, yo, k3, ssk, k3, k1 tbl, k3, k2tog, k3, yo, p1) to last 21 sts, k1 tbl, p1, yo, k3, ssk, k3, k1 tbl, k4, m1r, p1, k1 tbl, p1, k3. [1 st inc'd]

Row 30: K4, p1 tbl, k1, p5, p1 tbl, p2, ssp, p3, yo, p1, k1, p1 tbl, (k1, p1, yo, p3, p2tog, p2, p1 tbl, p2, ssp, p3, yo, p1, k1, p1 tbl) to last 4 sts, k4.

Row 31: K3, p1, (k1 tbl, p1, k2, yo, k3, ssk, k1, k1 tbl, k1, k2tog, k3, yo, k2, p1) to last 22 sts, k1 tbl, p1, k2, yo, k3, ssk, k1, k1 tbl, k5, m1r, p1, k1 tbl, p1, k3. [1 st inc'd]

Row 32: K4, p1 tbl, k1, p6, p1 tbl, ssp, p3, yo, p3, k1, p1 tbl, (k1, p3, yo, p3, p2tog, p1 tbl, ssp, p3, yo, p3, k1, p1 tbl) to last 4 sts, k4.

Row 33: K3, p1, (k1 tbl, p1, yo, k3, ssk, k3, k1 tbl, k3, k2tog, k3, yo, p1) to last 23 sts, k1 tbl, p1, yo, k3, ssk, k3, k1 tbl, k6, m1r, p1, k1 tbl, p1, k3. [1 st inc'd]

Row 34: K4, p1 tbl, k1, p7, p1 tbl, p2, ssp, p3, yo, p1, k1, p1 tbl, (k1, p1, yo, p3, p2tog, p2, p1 tbl, p2, ssp, p3, yo, p1, k1, p1 tbl) to last 4 sts, k4.

Row 35: K3, p1, (k1 tbl, p1, k2, yo, k3, ssk, k1, k1 tbl, k1, k2tog, k3, yo, k2, p1) to last 24 sts, k1 tbl, p1, k2, yo, k3, ssk, k1, k1 tbl, k7, m1r, p1, k1 tbl, p1, k3. [1 st inc'd]

Row 36: K4, p1 tbl, k1, p8, p1 tbl, ssp, p3, yo, p3, k1, p1 tbl, (k1, p3, yo, p3, p2tog, p1 tbl, ssp, p3, yo, p3, k1, p1 tbl) to last 4 sts, k4.

Row 37: K3, p1, (k1 tbl, p1, yo, k3, ssk, k3, k1 tbl, k3, k2tog, k3, yo, p1) to last 25 sts, k1 tbl, p1, yo, k3, ssk, k1 tbl, k3, k2tog, k3, yo, m1r, p1, k1 tbl, p1, k3. [1 st inc'd]

Row 38: K4, p1 tbl, k1, (k1, p1, yo, p3, p2tog, p2, p1 tbl, p2, ssp, p3, yo, p1, k1, p1 tbl) to last 4 sts, k4.

Row 39: K3, p1, (k1 tbl, p1, k2, yo, k3, ssk, k1, k1 tbl, k1, k2tog, k3, yo, k2, p1) to last 6 sts, m1r, p1, k1 tbl, p1, k3. [1 st inc'd]

Row 40: K4, p1 tbl, k1, p1 tbl, (k1, p3, yo, p3, p2tog, p1 tbl, ssp, p3, yo, p3, k1, p1 tbl) to last 4 sts, k4.

FINAL BORDER

Final border row (RS): K3, (p1, k1 tbl) to last 4 sts, p1, k3.

Final border row (WS): K3, (k1, p1 tbl) to last 4 sts, k4.

Work final border rows 3 times (6 rows total).

FLOWER STITCH CHART

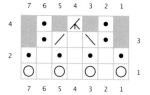

BINDING OFF

STITCH GUIDE

Bobble BO st: In the next st, (k1, k1 tbl) 3 times, pass 5 loops just created over the last loop created, pass the first st on the needle over the second st.

BO all sts the following way:

K2, (pass the first st on the needle over the second st, k1) 12 times, pass the first st on the needle over the second st, *work 1 bobble BO st, (k1, pass the first st on the needle over the second st) 9 times; repeat from * until all sts are bound off.

FINISHING

Cut yarn. Weave in ends. Block to the desired dimensions.

CHART KEY

	RS: knit WS: purl
•	RS: purl WS: knit
O	yo
\	RS: ssk WS: ssp
/	RS: ssp WS: ssk
⅄	WS: p3tog
Ω	RS: k tbl WS: p tbl
⌐	m1r
⌐	m1l
⚘	flower (work Flower Chart over these stitches)
▓	no stitch
	repeat

BODY CHART

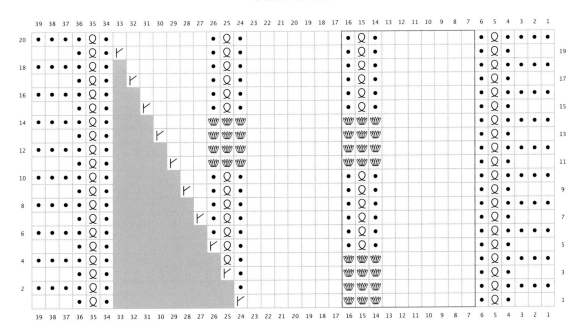

[continued]

SETUP CHART

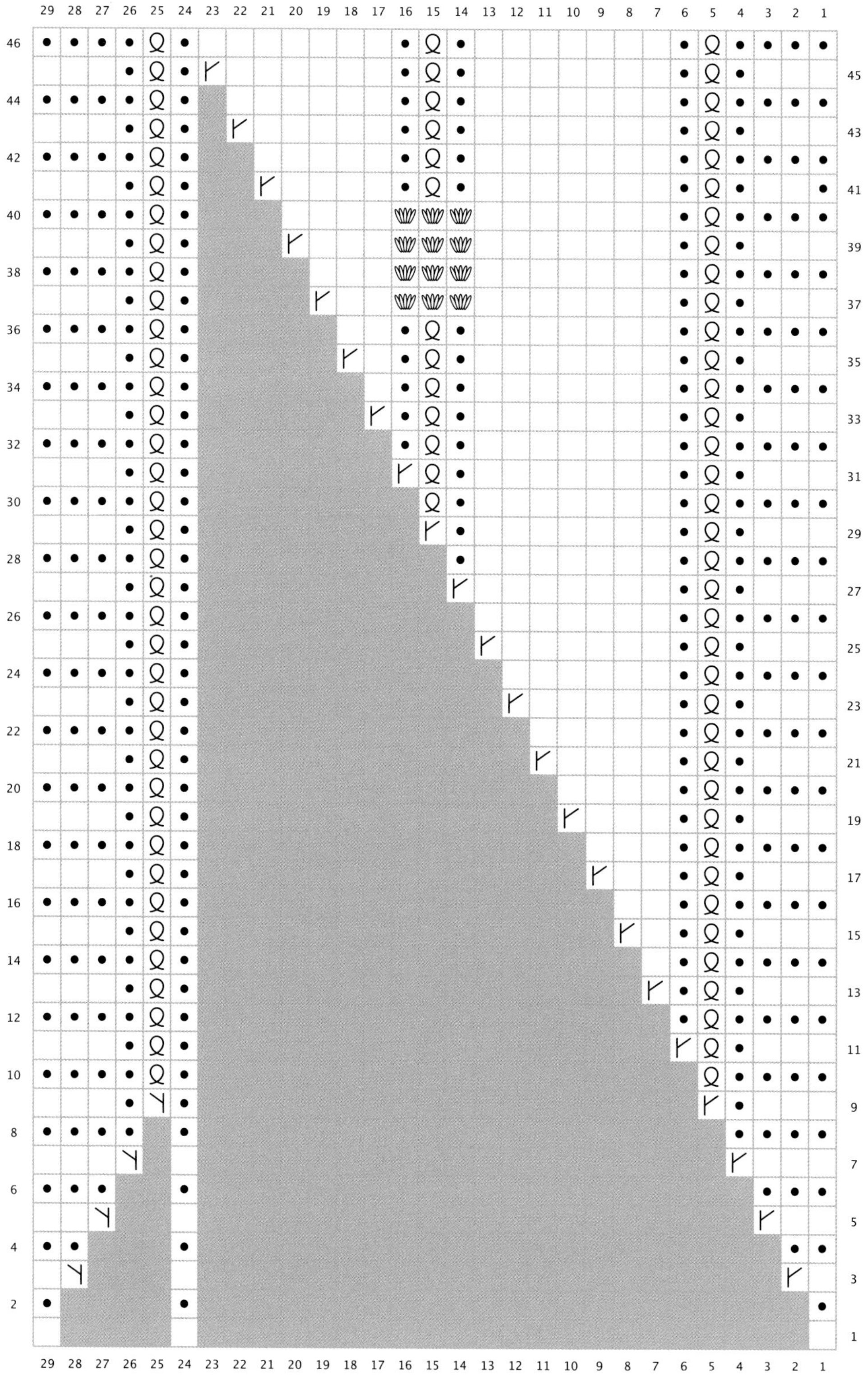
29 28 27 26 25 24 23 22 21 20 19 18 17 16 15 14 13 12 11 10 9 8 7 6 5 4 3 2 1
46 44 42 40 38 36 34 32 30 28 26 24 22 20 18 16 14 12 10 8 6 4 2
45 43 41 39 37 35 33 31 29 27 25 23 21 19 17 15 13 11 9 7 5 3 1

BORDER CHART

Lyrebird Socks

Birds, the aerial creatures that they are, are truly fascinating. The variety of their species, their beauty and their originality never cease to amaze me. Lyrebirds, for example, have two long feathers resembling vertebrae as a part of their tails. These socks have a similar pattern on the top of the feet, starting at the cuff and ending softly at the toes, so it was only appropriate to name them after their feathered inspiration.

Construction

These socks are worked from the cuff down. You'll knit the cuff first, followed by the leg, both of which are worked in the round. Afterward, the heel flap and heel turn are worked flat. Stitches are picked up along the edges of the flap to form the gusset, which is then worked in the round, followed by the foot and the toes. The lace stitch pattern is worked from the cuff to the toes, where cables are worked to close the pattern.

Skill Level: Intermediate

Sizes

* 1 (2, 3)

Finished Measurements

* **Finished leg circumference:** 7.5 (8, 9) inches / 19 (20.25, 23) cm, blocked

Materials

YARN

Fingering weight, Akara Yarns Merino Sock (80% superwash merino; 20% nylon), 420 yds (384 m) per 115-g skein

YARDAGE/METERAGE

278 (330, 406) yds / 254 (302, 371) m

SHOWN IN

Urban (1 skein)

NEEDLES

For ribbing: US 0 (2 mm), 32-inch (80-cm) circular needle for magic loop, DPNs, two circulars or 9-inch (23-cm) circular needle

For body of sock: US 2 (2.75 mm), 32-inch (80-cm) circular needle for magic loop, DPNs, two circulars or 9-inch (23-cm) circular needle

NOTIONS

3 stitch markers

2 removable markers

Cable needle

Tapestry needle

GAUGE

32 sts × 44 rows = 4 inches (10 cm) in stockinette stitch (blocked), with larger needles.

Important note: Take time to check your gauge. This will ensure correct fit and yarn quantity.

Special Techniques

German Twisted Cast-On (page 149)

[continued]

ABBREVIATIONS	
BOR	beginning of round
cdd	central double decrease
Cn	cable needle
CO	cast on
dec'd	decreased
k	knit
k2tog	knit two together
k3tog	knit three together
m	marker
m1r	make one right
m1l	make one left
p	purl
p2tog	purl two together
pm	place marker
rem	remaining
rm	remove marker
rnd(s)	round(s)
RS	right side
sl	slip
sm	slip marker
ssk	slip slip knit
sssk	slip slip slip knit
st(s)	stitch(es)
tbl	through back loop
WS	wrong side
wyif	with yarn in front
yo	yarn over
1/2 LC	1/2 Left Cable: Sl 1 to Cn, hold to front, k2; k1 tbl from Cn
1/2 RC	1/2 Right Cable: Sl 2 to Cn, hold to back, k1 tbl; k2 from Cn
3/2 LC	3/2 Left Cable: Sl 3 to Cn, hold to front, k2; (k1 tbl, p1, k1 tbl) from Cn
3/2 RC	3/2 Right Cable: Sl 2 to Cn, hold to back, k1 tbl, p1, k1 tbl; k2 from Cn

Lyrebird Socks Pattern

Both socks are worked alike.

You may work these socks either from the charts (page 119) or from the written instructions. Look for the separate sections as you proceed through the pattern.

With smaller needles, CO 60 (64, 72) sts using the German Twisted Cast-On.

Pm to indicate BOR and join to work in the round.

CUFF

Work in twisted ribbing for 1 inch (2.5 cm), as follows:

Twisted ribbing (size 1): (K1 tbl, p1) around.

Twisted ribbing (sizes 2–3): (P 1, k1 tbl) around.

LEG

Switch to larger needles.

Work either from the written or chart instructions that follow until the leg measures approximately 7 (7.5, 8) inches / 17.75 (19, 20.25) cm from the CO edge, ending with rnd 4 of chart or leg rnd 4. Then proceed to **Heel Flap** (page 117).

WRITTEN INSTRUCTIONS

Leg rnd 1: K 36 (39, 45), k tbl, p1, k tbl, p2, k9, p2, k tbl, p1, k tbl, k to end.

Leg rnd 2: Repeat leg rnd 1.

Leg rnd 3: K 36 (39, 45), k tbl, p1, k tbl, p2, k3tog, (yo, k1) 3 times, yo, sssk, p2, k tbl, p1, k tbl, k to end.

Leg rnd 4: Repeat leg rnd 1.

CHART INSTRUCTIONS

Leg rnd: K 36 (39, 45), work Leg Chart over 19 sts, k to end.

HEEL FLAP

Rm and place first 31 (33, 37) sts onto one needle. Heel flap will be worked back and forth in rows on these sts. The rem 29 (31, 35) sts will be worked later for instep.

Heel flap row (RS): Sl1, (p1, sl1) to end.

Heel flap row (WS): Sl1 wyif, (k1, p1 tbl) to end.

Work a total of 28 (32, 36) heel flap rows.

HEEL TURN

Work short rows as follows:

Short row 1 (RS): Sl1, k 19 (21, 23), ssk, k1, turn work.

Short row 2 (WS): Sl1, p 10 (12, 12), p2tog, p1, turn work.

Short row 3: Sl1, k to 1 st before the gap, ssk, k1, turn work.

Short row 4: Sl1, p to 1 st before the gap, p2tog, p1, turn work.

Repeat short rows 3–4 until all sts have been worked; 21 (23, 25) sts remain.

Next row (RS): K all heel sts.

GUSSET

Work either from the written or chart instructions that follow to work a total of 21 (25, 27) rows (including the setup row). Then proceed to the **Foot** (page 118).

WRITTEN INSTRUCTIONS

Setup Row: Pick up and k 15 (17, 19) sts along the edge of heel flap, pm, k 5 (6, 8), k tbl, p1, k tbl, p2, k9, p2, k tbl, p1, k tbl, k 5 (6, 8), pm, pick up and k 15 (17, 19) sts along heel flap, k 10 (11, 12), pm to indicate BOR (located at the center of heel). [80 (88, 98) sts]

Start working in the round.

Rnd 1: K to m, sm, k 5 (6, 8), k tbl, p1, k tbl, p2, k9, p2, k tbl, p1, k tbl, k 5 (6, 8), sm, k to end.

Rnd 2: K to 3 sts before m, k2tog, k1, sm, k 5 (6, 8), k tbl, p1, k tbl, p2, k3tog, (yo, k1) 3 times, yo, sssk, p2, k tbl, p1, k tbl, k 5 (6, 8), sm, k1, ssk, k to end. [2 sts dec'd]

Rnd 3: Repeat rnd 1.

Rnd 4: K to 3 sts before m, k2tog, k1, sm, k 5 (6, 8), k tbl, p1, k tbl, p2, k9, p2, k tbl, p1, k tbl, k 5 (6, 8), sm, k1, ssk, k to end. [2 sts dec'd]

Work rnds 1–4 for a total of 20 (24, 26) rnds, ending with rnd 4 (4, 2). [60 (64, 72) sts]

CHART INSTRUCTIONS

Setup Row: Pick up and k 15 (17, 19) sts along the edge of heel flap, pm, k 5 (6, 8), work first row of chart over 19 sts, k 5 (6, 8), pm, pick up and k 15 (17, 19) sts along heel flap, k 10 (11, 12), pm to indicate BOR (located at the center of heel). [80 (88, 98) sts]

Start working in the round.

Rnd 1: K to m, sm, k 5 (6, 8), work next row of chart over 19 sts, k 5 (6, 8), sm, k to end.

Rnd 2: K to 3 sts before m, k2tog, k1, sm, k 5 (6, 8), work next row of chart over 19 sts, k 5 (6, 8), sm, k1, ssk, k to end. [2 sts dec'd]

Work rnds 1–2 a total of 10 (12, 13) times. [60 (64, 72) sts]

[continued]

FOOT

Work either from the written or chart instructions that follow until the piece measures approximately 7 (8, 9) inches / 18 (20.25, 23) cm from back of heel or 2 (2, 2.25) inches / 5 (5, 5.5) cm less than the desired length, ending with rnd 4 of chart or foot rnd 4. Then proceed to **Shaping Toes**.

WRITTEN INSTRUCTIONS

Work as follows, starting foot rnd 2 (2, 4) and ending foot rnd 4.

Foot rnd 1: K to m, sm, k 5 (6, 8), k tbl, p1, k tbl, p2, k9, p2, k tbl, p1, k tbl, k 5 (6, 8), sm, k to end.

Foot rnd 2: Repeat rnd 1.

Foot rnd 3: K to m, sm, k 5 (6, 8), K tbl, p1, k tbl, p2, k3tog, (yo, k1) 3 times, yo, sssk, p2, k tbl, p1, k tbl, k 5 (6, 8), sm, k to end.

Foot rnd 4: Repeat rnd 1.

CHART INSTRUCTIONS

Foot rnd: K to m, sm, k 5 (6, 8), work next row of chart over 19 sts, k 5 (6, 8), sm, k to end.

SHAPING TOES

Remove markers, keeping only BOR marker.

Work either from the written or chart instructions that follow for 9 rnds to start working the toes and to end the lace pattern. Then proceed to **Ending Toes** (page 119).

On every other rnd, starting at the rnd following the setup rnd, markers around the lace pattern will be moved closer together; you will be moving the marker located before the pattern 2 sts forward and the marker located after the pattern 2 sts backward.

WRITTEN INSTRUCTIONS

Setup rnd: K 13 (14, 16), k2tog, k1, pm, k1, ssk, k 2 (3, 5), place removable m, 3/2 LC, k9, 3/2 RC, place removable m, k 2 (3, 5), k2tog, k1, pm, k1, ssk, k to end. [56 (60, 68) sts]

Toe rnd 1: K to second m, rm, k2, replace m, k tbl, p1, k tbl, k9, k tbl, p1, k tbl, move next removable m to this spot (2 sts backward), k to end.

Toe rnd 2: K to 3 sts before m, k2tog, k1, sm, k1, ssk, k to next m, sm, 3/2 LC, k2tog, yo, k1, yo, ssk, 3/2 RC, sm, k to 3 sts before m, k2tog, k1, sm, k1, ssk, k to end. [4 sts dec'd]

Toe rnd 3: K to second m, rm, k2, replace m, k tbl, p1, k tbl, k5, k tbl, p1, k tbl, move next removable m to this spot (2 sts backward), k to end.

Toe rnd 4: K to 3 sts before m, k2tog, k1, sm, k1, ssk, k to next m, sm, 3/2 LC, k1, 3/2 RC, sm, k to 3 sts before m, k2tog, k1, sm, k1, ssk, k to end. [4 sts dec'd]

Toe rnd 5: K to second m, rm, k2, replace m, k tbl, p1, k tbl, k1, k tbl, p1, k tbl, move next removable m to this spot (2 sts backward), k to end.

Toe rnd 6: K to 3 sts before m, k2tog, k1, sm, k1, ssk, k to next m, sm, 1/2 LC, k1, 1/2 RC, sm, k to 3 sts before m, k2tog, k1, sm, k1, ssk, k to end. [4 sts dec'd]

Toe rnd 7: K to second m, rm, k2, replace m, k tbl, k1, k tbl, move next removable m to this spot (2 sts backward), k to end.

Toe rnd 8: K to 3 sts before m, k2tog, k1, sm, k1, ssk, k to next m, rm, m1r, cdd, m1l, rm, k to 3 sts before m, k2tog, k1, sm, k1, ssk, k to end. [4 sts dec'd]

CHART INSTRUCTIONS

Setup rnd: K 13 (14, 16), k2tog, k1, pm, k1, ssk, k 2 (3, 5), place removable m, work from Toe Chart over 19 sts, place removable m, k 2 (3, 5), k2tog, k1, pm, k1, ssk, k to end. [56 (60, 68) sts]

Toe rnd 1: K to second m, rm, k2, replace m, work from Toe Chart to last 2 sts before next removable m, move next removable m to this spot (2 sts backward), k to end.

Toe rnd 2: K to 3 sts before m, k2tog, k1, sm, k1, ssk, k to next m, sm, work from Toe Chart to next m, sm, k to 3 sts before m, k2tog, k1, sm, k1, ssk, k to end. [4 sts dec'd]

Work toe rnds 1–2 a total of 4 times to complete the chart. [40 (44, 52) sts]

On the last rnd, remove markers around the lace pattern.

ENDING TOES

Toe ending rnd 1: K all sts.

Toe ending rnd 2: (K to 3 sts before m, k2tog, k1, sm, k1, ssk) twice, k to end. [4 sts dec'd]

Work toe ending rnds 1–2 a total of 4 (4, 5) times. [24 (28, 32) sts]

Work toe ending rnd 2 only, 3 (4, 5) more times. [12 (12, 12) sts]

FINISHING

Cut yarn, leaving a 6-inch (15-cm) tail. Thread yarn through rem sts. Weave in all ends, block to the desired dimensions.

CHART KEY

☐	knit
•	purl
Ⴓ	k tbl
/	k2tog
\	ssk
⋏	k3tog
⋋	sssk
⋀	cdd
O	yo
⌐	m1r
⌐	m1l
⤬	1/2 Left Cable: Sl 1 to cn, hold to front, k2; k1 tbl from cn
⤬	1/2 Right Cable: Sl 2 to cn, hold to back, k1 tbl; k2 from cn
⤬	3/2 Right Cable: Sl 2 to cn, hold to front, k2; (k1 tbl, p1, k1 tbl) from cn
⤬	3/2 Left Cable: Sl3 to cn, hold to front, k2; (k1 tbl, p1, k1 tbl) from cn
▨	no stitch

LEG CHART

```
19 18 17 16 15 14 13 12 11 10  9  8  7  6  5  4  3  2  1
Ⴓ  •  Ⴓ  •  •                             •  •  Ⴓ  •  Ⴓ   4
Ⴓ  •  Ⴓ  •  • ⋋  O        O        O  O ⋏ •  •  Ⴓ  •  Ⴓ   3
Ⴓ  •  Ⴓ  •  •                             •  •  Ⴓ  •  Ⴓ   2
Ⴓ  •  Ⴓ  •  •                             •  •  Ⴓ  •  Ⴓ   1
19 18 17 16 15 14 13 12 11 10  9  8  7  6  5  4  3  2  1
```

TOE CHART

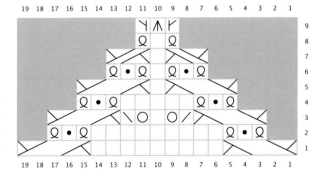

The Luminous Collection

Joyful Designs to Knit Cheerfully

Knitting shouldn't be praised only for the warmth it provides. If our minds often associate knitting with bulky sweaters and warm hats, a great variety of projects are perfect for warmer days—and I'm sure that a lot of knitters agree that our craft is a four-season practice! Lighter projects feel as festive as a picnic in a park, as pretty as a sunset over the sea.

The *Luminous* Collection was designed to celebrate the warmth of the sun in a happy, knitted way. The Solstice Top (page 123) is proof that wearing knitted garments is just as great when it's warm outside as it is when the snow blows, while the Soft Breeze Shawl (page 132) and the Meadow Socks (page 144) are classic accessories for warm weather. The Filigree Scrunchie (page 141), on the other hand, is an original project that I hope will inspire you to employ knitting beyond its traditional applications.

Solstice Top

When I think of the summer solstice, I imagine the first day of summer being filled with kisses of warm air on my still untanned skin while the sun celebrates its favorite season by offering its presence for longer than usual. On that day, the joyful energy feels like the promise of a season filled with special moments that are sure to form memories to keep the heart warm during the colder months. Lively summers and a warm sense of happiness inspired this design. The Solstice Top is a joyful garment with some sweet details: a rolling edge at the neckline, slightly puffed sleeves against drop shoulders and a lace panel embellished with bobbles. With its loose fit and top-down construction, which allows the knitter to make either a long top or a cropped one, this simple tee is flattering on bodies of all shapes and sizes.

Construction

This top is worked from the top down, almost seamlessly, with a simple drop-shoulder construction. The front shoulder pieces are worked first, then joined together where the front lace panel begins. The front piece is worked down to the underarms and put on hold. The back piece is worked in one piece, from the top down to the underarms. The front and back pieces are then joined and the top is worked in the round from that point evenly, ending with a ribbing section. The shoulders are sewn together, and the sleeves start by picking up stitches in a way that creates a little puffed shoulder. They are then worked top-down in the round. The sleeve width is decreased before working the final ribbing. Finally, the neckline stitches are picked up and a rolling edge is worked.

Skill Level: Intermediate

Sizes

* 1 (2, 3, 4) (5, 6, 7, 8) (9, 10, 11, 12)

Finished Measurements

* **Finished bust:** 32.25 (33.75, 36, 38.25) (40.25, 43.5, 46.25, 49.25) (52, 55.25, 58.5, 61) inches / 82 (85.5, 91.5, 97) (102, 110.5, 117.5, 125) (132, 140.5, 148.5, 155) cm

* **Recommended ease:** To be worn with approximately 2–5 inches (5–13 cm) of positive ease. Pick a size larger than your bust circumference. Sample shown is knit in size 3, worn with 2 inches (5 cm) of ease.

Materials

YARN

Light fingering or fingering weight, Malabrigo Sock (100% superwash merino wool), 440 yds (402 m) per 100-g skein

YARDAGE/METERAGE

789 (854, 934, 1006) (1088, 1206, 1354, 1456) (1587, 1722, 1895, 1987) yds / 721 (781, 854, 920) (995, 1103, 1238, 1331) (1451, 1575, 1733, 1817) m

Note: The indicated yardage will create a garment that hits at the top of the hips. The length is customizable. Plan for more yardage to achieve a longer top.

SHOWN IN

803 Ochre [2 (2, 3, 3) (3, 3, 4, 4) (4, 4, 5, 5) skeins]

(continued)

NEEDLES

For body: US 2 (2.75 mm), 24- to 32-inch (60- to 80-cm) circular needle

For sleeves: US 1 (2.25 mm), 12-inch (30-cm) circular needle or DPNs

For neckline: US 1 (2.25 mm), 16-inch (40-cm) circular needle

NOTIONS

3 stitch markers

Tapestry needle

2 stitch holders or waste yarn

Crochet hook (to make bobbles)

Gauge

30 sts × 34 rows = 4 inches (10 cm) in stockinette stitch using larger needle (blocked)

Important note: Take time to check your gauge. This will ensure correct fit and yarn quantity.

Special Technique

Bobbles (page 152): For this pattern, I recommend doing 5 repetitions of (k1, yo) in the same stitch.

ABBREVIATIONS	
BO	bind off
CO	cast on
dec('d)	decrease(d)
inc'd	increased
k	knit
k2tog	knit two together
k3tog	knit three together
m	marker
mb	make bobble
m1l	make one left
m1r	make one right
p	purl
pm	place marker
RS	right side
ssk	slip slip knit
sssk	slip slip slip knit
st(s)	stitch(es)
WS	wrong side
yo	yarn over

Stitch Patterns

LACE PANEL (WORKED FLAT)

Row 1 (RS): (P1, k3) twice, p1, k5, yo, k2, ssk, k2, p1, k2, k2tog, k2, yo, k5, (p1, k3) twice, p1.

Row 2 (WS): (K1, p3) twice, (k1, p11) twice, (k1, p3) twice, k1.

Row 3: P1, k3tog, yo, p1, k3, p1, k6, yo, k2, ssk, k1, p1, k1, k2tog, k2, yo, k6, p1, k3, p1, yo, sssk, p1. [2 sts dec'd]

Row 4: K1, p1, yo, p1, k1, p3, (k1, p11) twice, k1, p3, k1, p1, yo, p1, k1. [2 sts inc'd]

Row 5: (P1, k3) twice, p1, k7, yo, k2, ssk, p1, k2tog, k2, yo, k7, (p1, k3) twice, p1.

Row 6: Repeat row 2.

Row 7: P1, k3tog, yo, p1, k3, (p1, k11) twice, p1, k3, p1, yo, sssk, p1. [2 sts dec'd]

Row 8: Repeat row 4. [2 sts inc'd]

Row 9: (P1, k3) twice, p1, k1, (yo, k2, ssk) twice, k2, p1, k2, (k2tog, k2, yo) twice, k1, (p1, k3) twice, p1.

Row 10: Repeat row 2.

Row 11: P1, k3tog, yo, p1, k3, p1, k2, (yo, k2, ssk) twice, k1, p1, k1, (k2tog, k2, yo) twice, k2, p1, k3, p1, yo, sssk, p1. [2 sts dec'd]

Row 12: Repeat row 4.

Row 13: (P1, k3) 3 times, (yo, k2, ssk) twice, p1, (k2tog, k2, yo) twice, (k3, p1) 3 times.

Row 14: Repeat row 2.

Row 15: P1, k3tog, yo, p1, k3, p1, k4, yo, k2, ssk, k3, p1, k3, k2tog, k2, yo, k4, p1, k3, p1, yo, sssk, p1. [2 sts dec'd]

Row 16: Repeat row 4.

Row 17: (P1, k3) twice, mb, k5, yo, k2, ssk, k2, p1, k2, k2tog, k2, yo, k5, mb, (k3, p1) twice.

Row 18: Repeat row 2.

Row 19: P1, k3tog, yo, p1, k1, mb, k1, p1, k1, mb, k4, yo, k2, ssk, k1, p1, k1, k2tog, k2, yo, k4, mb, k1, p1, k1, mb, k1, p1, yo, sssk, p1. [2 sts dec'd]

Row 20: Repeat row 4. [2 sts inc'd]

Row 21: (P1, k3) twice, mb, k7, yo, k2, ssk, p1, k2tog, k2, yo, k7, mb, (k3, p1) twice.

Row 22: Repeat row 2.

Row 23: Repeat row 7.

Row 24: Repeat row 4.

LACE PANEL (WORKED IN THE ROUND)

Rnd 1: (P1, k3) twice, p1, k5, yo, k2, ssk, k2, p1, k2, k2tog, k2, yo, k5, (p1, k3) twice, p1.

Rnd 2: (P1, k3) twice, (p1, k11) twice, (p1, k3) twice, p1.

Rnd 3: P1, k3tog, yo, p1, k3, p1, k6, yo, k2, ssk, k1, p1, k1, k2tog, k2, yo, k6, p1, k3, p1, yo, sssk, p1. [2 sts dec'd]

Rnd 4: P1, k1, yo, k1, p1, k3, (p1, k11) twice, p1, k3, p1, k1, yo, k1, p1. [2 sts inc'd]

Rnd 5: (P1, k3) twice, p1, k7, yo, k2, ssk, p1, k2tog, k2, yo, k7, (p1, k3) twice, p1.

Rnd 6: Repeat rnd 2.

Rnd 7: P1, k3tog, yo, p1, k3, (p1, k11) twice, p1, k3, p1, yo, sssk, p1. [2 sts dec'd]

Rnd 8: Repeat rnd 4. [2 sts inc'd]

Rnd 9: (P1, k3) twice, p1, k1, (yo, k2, ssk) twice, k2, p1, k2, (k2tog, k2, yo) twice, k1, (p1, k3) twice, p1.

Rnd 10: Repeat rnd 2.

Rnd 11: P1, k3tog, yo, p1, k3, p1, k2, (yo, k2, ssk) twice, k1, p1, k1, (k2tog, k2, yo) twice, k2, p1, k3, p1, yo, sssk, p1. [2 sts dec'd]

Rnd 12: Repeat rnd 4. [2 sts inc'd]

Rnd 13: (P1, k3) 3 times, (yo, k2, ssk) twice, p1, (k2tog, k2, yo) twice, (k3, p1) 3 times.

Rnd 14: Repeat rnd 2.

Rnd 15: P1, k3tog, yo, p1, k3, p1, k4, yo, k2, ssk, k3, p1, k3, k2tog, k2, yo, k4, p1, k3, p1, yo, sssk, p1. [2 sts dec'd]

Rnd 16: Repeat rnd 4.

Rnd 17: (P1, k3) twice, mb, k5, yo, k2, ssk, k2, p1, k2, k2tog, k2, yo, k5, mb, (k3, p1) twice.

[continued]

Rnd 18: Repeat rnd 2.

Rnd 19: P1, k3tog, yo, p1, k1, mb, k1, p1, k1, mb, k4, yo, k2, ssk, k1, p1, k1, k2tog, k2, yo, k4, mb, k1, p1, k1, mb, k1, p1, yo, sssk, p1. [2 sts dec'd]

Rnd 20: Repeat rnd 4. [2 sts inc'd]

Rnd 21: (P1, k3) twice, mb, k7, yo, k2, ssk, p1, k2tog, k2, yo, k7, mb, (k3, p1) twice.

Rnd 22: Repeat rnd 2.

Rnd 23: Repeat rnd 7.

Rnd 24: Repeat rnd 4.

Pattern Notes

- Left and right indications refer to the wearer's side.

- You may choose to work the lace patterns from the charts (pages 130–131) or the preceding written text.

- Your stitch count will vary in the lace panels: 2 stitches are decreased in rows 3, 7, 11, 15, 19 and 23 and added back in the following row.

Solstice Top Pattern

LEFT SHOULDER

CO 26 (28, 30, 34) (37, 41, 45, 48) (52, 56, 60, 63) sts.

Setup row (WS): P all sts.

Left shoulder row 1 (RS): K all sts.

Left shoulder row 2 (WS): P all sts.

Work both left shoulder rows 6 (6, 4, 6) (5, 4, 3, 3) (2, 2, 0, 0) times total, for a total of 12 (12, 8, 12) (10, 8, 6, 6) (4, 4, 0, 0) rows.

Shaping row 1 (RS): K1, m1l, k to end. [1 st inc'd]

Shaping row 2 (WS): P all sts.

Work both shaping rows 14 (15, 17, 16) (17, 19, 20, 21) (22, 24, 26, 27) times total, for a total of 28 (30, 34, 32) (34, 38, 40, 42) (44, 48, 52, 54) rows.

[40 (43, 47, 50) (54, 60, 65, 69) (74, 80, 86, 90) sts]

Cut yarn, place sts on holder.

RIGHT SHOULDER

CO 26 (28, 30, 34) (37, 41, 45, 48) (52, 56, 60, 63) sts.

Setup row (WS): P all sts.

Right shoulder row 1 (RS): K all sts.

Right shoulder row 2 (WS): P all sts.

Work both right shoulder rows 6 (6, 4, 6) (5, 4, 3, 3) (2, 2, 0, 0) times total, for a total of 12 (12, 8, 12) (10, 8, 6, 6) (4, 4, 0, 0) rows.

Shaping row 1 (RS): K to last st, m1r, k1. [1 st inc'd]

Shaping row 2 (WS): P all sts.

Work both shaping rows 14 (15, 17, 16) (17, 19, 20, 21) (22, 24, 26, 27) times total, for a total of 28 (30, 34, 32) (34, 38, 40, 42) (44, 48, 52, 54) rows.

[**St count:** 40 (43, 47, 50) (54, 60, 65, 69) (74, 80, 86, 90) sts]

JOINING FRONT PIECES

- -

Note: Use the cable cast-on method to cast on stitches in the joining row.

- -

Joining row (RS): K all sts from right shoulder, CO 41 (41, 41, 43) (43, 43, 43, 47) (47, 47, 47, 49) sts, k all sts from left shoulder. [121 (127, 135, 143) (151, 163, 173, 185) (195, 207, 219, 229) sts]

Setup Row (WS): P 40 (43, 47, 51) (55, 61, 66, 72) (77, 83, 89, 94), pm, p 41, pm, p to end.

FRONT PIECE

Front piece RS Row: K 40 (43, 47, 51) (55, 61, 66, 72) (77, 83, 89, 94), work lace panel (worked flat) between markers, k to end.

Front piece WS Row: P 40 (43, 47, 51) (55, 61, 66, 72) (77, 83, 89, 94), work lace panel (worked flat) between markers, p to end.

Work both front piece rows 15 (17, 17, 18) (18, 20, 23, 23) (24, 25, 27, 27) times total, for a total of 30 (34, 34, 36) (36, 40, 46, 46) (48, 50, 54, 54) rows, repeating lace panel rows as required.

Make note of the lace panel row that you end with, so that you are sure to end the back piece on the same row.

Cut yarn, place sts on holder.

BACK PIECE

CO 121 (127, 135, 143) (151, 163, 173, 185) (195, 207, 219, 229) sts.

Setup row (WS): P all sts.

Back piece RS row: K all sts.

Back piece WS row: P all sts.

Work both back piece rows 35 (38, 38, 40) (40, 43, 46, 47) (48, 51, 53, 54) times total, for a total of 70 (76, 76, 80) (80, 86, 92, 94) (96, 102, 106, 108) rows.

Cut yarn.

JOINING BACK AND FRONT

Place the front piece back on the needles, before the back piece. Join yarn at the front piece. Continue working the lace panel beginning on the next row.

Joining row (RS): K 40 (43, 47, 51) (55, 61, 66, 72) (77, 83, 89, 94), work lace panel between markers, k to end of front piece, k all sts from back piece.

[**St count at bust:** 242 (254, 270, 286) (302, 326, 346, 370) (390, 414, 438, 458) sts]

Pm and join to work in the round.

BODY

Body rnd: K 40 (43, 47, 51) (55, 61, 66, 72) (77, 83, 89, 94), work lace panel (worked in the round) between markers, k to end.

Work in body rnd until body measures 11 (11, 11.5, 11.5) (12, 12, 12.5, 12.5) (13, 13, 13.5, 13.5) inches / 28 (28, 29, 29) (30.5, 30.5, 32, 32) (33, 33, 34.5, 34.5) cm or the desired length from underarm.

[continued]

BOTTOM RIBBING

Switch to smaller needles.

Ribbing rnd: (K1, p1) around.

Work in ribbing rnd until ribbing measures 1 inch (2.5 cm).

BO all sts in pattern.

SEWING SHOULDERS

Place back and front piece with the right sides facing together, aligning the top of shoulders together (CO edge of both front and back). Using a 20-inch (51-cm) strand of yarn, sew back and front pieces together, working across all sts from the front CO edges.

SLEEVES

With larger needles, pick up and k 110 (118, 118, 124) (124, 134, 142, 146) (150, 158, 164, 166) sts around the opening, picking up 53 (57, 57, 60) (60, 65, 69, 71) (73, 77, 80, 81) sts on each side and 4 sts from the joining row, the following way:

Starting at underarm, pick up and k 4 sts from joining row, placing a m after the second st;

Pick up and k 35 (38, 38, 40) (40, 43, 46, 47) (46, 51, 53, 54) sts, picking up approximately 2 sts out of 3 rows along the lower part of the opening;

Pick up 18 (19, 19, 20) (20, 22, 23, 24) (27, 26, 27, 27) sts, picking up approximately 1 st for each row up to the shoulder seam;

Keep picking up sts on the other side of the opening, picking up 18 (19, 19, 20) (20, 22, 23, 24) (27, 26, 27, 27) sts (approximately 1 st for each row) close to the shoulder, and 35 (38, 38, 40) (40, 43, 46, 47) (46, 51, 53, 54) sts on the lower part of the opening (pick up approximately 2 sts out of 3 rows).

[110 (118, 118, 124) (124, 134, 142, 146) (150, 158, 164, 166) sts]

Join to work in the round and k up to m.

K all sts for 16 (12, 20, 18) (22, 16, 18, 28) (36, 36, 36, 34) rnds.

Dec rnd 1: K1, k2tog, k to last 3 sts, ssk, k1. [2 sts dec'd]

Dec rnd 2: K all sts.

Work both dec rnds 6 (8, 5, 6) (5, 8, 8, 3) (0, 0, 1, 2) times total, for a total of 12 (16, 10, 12) (10, 16, 16, 6) (0, 0, 2, 4) rnds.

[98 (102, 108, 112) (114, 118, 126, 140) (150, 158, 162, 162) sts]

Next rnd (dec): (K10 (10, 11, 12) (12, 12, 13, 15) (16, 17, 18, 18), k2tog) to last 2 (6, 4, 0) (2, 6, 6, 4) (6, 6, 2, 2) sts, k to end.

[90 (94, 100, 104) (106, 110, 118, 132) (142, 150, 154, 154) sts]

Switch to smaller needles.

Work in (k1, p1) ribbing for 6 rnds.

BO all sts in pattern loosely.

NECKBAND

With smaller needles, starting at the left shoulder seam on front, pick up and knit approximately 2 sts out of 3 rows from the left shoulder piece, 9 sts out of 10 CO sts from the joining row, 2 sts out of 3 rows from the right shoulder piece and 9 sts out of 10 back CO sts.

Pm and join to work in the round.

K all sts for 6 rnds.

BO all sts knitwise.

FINISHING

Weave in all ends and block to the desired dimensions.

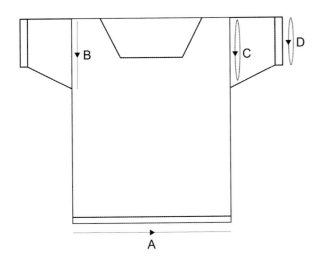

A: CIRCUMFERENCE AT BUST, WAIST, AND HIPS

32.25 (33.75, 36, 38.25) (40.25, 43.5, 46.25, 49.25) (52, 55.25, 58.5, 61) inches

82 (85.5, 91.5, 97) (102, 110.5, 117.5, 125) (132, 140.5, 148.5, 155) cm

B: ARMHOLE DEPTH

8.25 (9, 9, 9.5) (9.5, 10, 10.75, 11) (11.25, 12, 12.5, 12.75) inches

21 (23, 23, 24) (24, 25.5, 27.5, 28) (28.5, 30.5, 32, 32.5) cm

C: SLEEVES CIRCUMFERENCE AT TOP ARM

14.75 (15.75, 15.75, 16.5) (16.5, 17.75, 19, 19.5) (20, 21, 21.75, 22.25) inches

37.5 (40, 40, 42) (42, 45, 48.5, 49.5) (51, 53.5, 55.5, 56.5) cm

D: SLEEVES CIRCUMFERENCE AT RIBBING

12 (12.5, 13.25, 13.75) (14.25, 14.75, 15.75, 17.5) (19, 20, 20.5, 20.5) inches

30.5 (32, 33.5, 35) (36, 37.5, 40, 44.5) (48.5, 51, 52, 52) cm

CHART KEY

	RS: knit WS: purl
•	RS: purl WS: knit
O	yo
\	ssk
/	k2tog
⋏	k3tog
⋏	sssk
⓪	bobble
	no stitch

[continued]

LACE PANEL CHART
(WORKED FLAT)

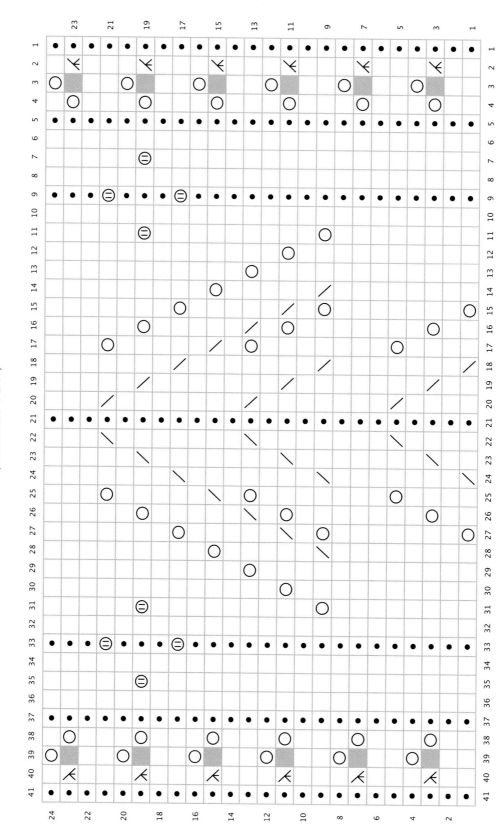

LACE PANEL CHART
(WORKED IN THE ROUND)

Soft Breeze Shawl

This dainty shawl gently mixes various techniques to create an elegant and playful accessory that will keep your neck and shoulders warm when a soft summer breeze is around. The body of the shawl is worked in garter stitch, with a variegated colorway (or not!), and it fades to the second—tonal or solid—colorway that is used to work the border. The lacy border features a pattern that looks like butterflies and an openwork pattern that grows at every row to create a frilly edge.

Construction

This triangular shawl is worked from the top down, growing by increasing at each edge and around the middle stitch. It is worked in garter stitch with the first color, then it fades to the second color by working stripes in the garter stitch section. The border is worked with the second color: the butterfly pattern first, followed by the growing eyelet pattern.

Skill Level: Intermediate

Sizes

- One size for adults

Finished Measurements

- 52 inches (132 cm) wide at top edge and 22 inches (56 cm) high at point, blocked

Materials

YARN
Fingering weight, Miss Babs Caroline (70% superwash merino wool; 20% cashmere; 10% nylon), 400 yds (365 m) per 95-g skein

YARDAGE/METERAGE
Color A: 230 yds / 210 m
Color B: 288 yds / 263 m

SHOWN IN
Color A: Rosy Finch (1 skein)
Color B: Dark Adobe (1 skein)

Any laceweight to DK weight yarn can be used for this pattern. Gauge, yardage and final size will vary. The shawl can also be made with only one color.

NEEDLES
US 3 (3.25 mm), 32-inch (80-cm) circular needle, or size needed to obtain gauge

NOTIONS
4 stitch markers
2 cable needles
Tapestry needle

(continued)

Gauge

24 sts × 46 rows = 4 inches (10 cm) in garter stitch (blocked)

26 sts × 36 rows = 4 inches (10 cm) in lace pattern (blocked)

Important note: Gauge can vary according to your yarn and needle size. If your gauge differs, your shawl will have different dimensions from the prototype. Make sure to plan for enough yardage.

ABBREVIATIONS	
BO	bind off
Cn	cable needle
CO	cast on
inc'd	increased
k	knit
k2tog	knit two together
m	marker
p	purl
pm	place marker
RS	right side
sl	slip
sm	slip marker
ssk	slip slip knit
st(s)	stitch(es)
WS	wrong side
yo	yarn over
2/2/2 RPC	2/2/2 right purl cable sl 2 sts to Cn placed behind the work, sl 2 sts on a second Cn placed behind, between the first Cn and the work, k2, p2 from second Cn, k2 from first Cn.

Soft Breeze Shawl Pattern

You may work this shawl either from the charts or from the written instructions. Look for the separate sections as you proceed through the pattern.

SETUP

With Color A, CO 3 sts.

K all sts for 10 rows.

Next row (RS): K3, do not turn, pm, pick up and k 5 sts along the edge, pm, pick up and k 3 sts from CO sts. [11 sts]

Next row (WS): K3, sm, k2, pm, k1 (middle st), pm, k2, sm, k3.

BODY

Body row (RS): K3, sm, yo, k to m, yo, sm, k1, sm, yo, k to last 3 sts, yo, sm, k3. [4 sts inc'd]

Body row (WS): K all sts.

Work body rows 55 times total (110 rows total). [231 sts: 3 border sts, 112 sts on the wing, 1 middle st, 112 sts on the wing, 3 border sts]

- -

Note: You can work a different number of rows, as long as you are ending with a multiple of 16 sts on each wing (a multiple of 32 + 7 sts for the whole shawl). [3 border sts, a multiple of 16 sts on the wing, 1 middle st, a multiple of 16 sts on the wing, 3 border sts]

- -

FADING SECTION

Create stripes while working 16 more body rows, starting with a RS row worked with Color A and changing color at each WS row: work row 1 with Color A, rows 2–3 with Color B, rows 4–5 with Color A, rows 6–7 with Color B and so on. [263 sts: 3 border sts, 128 sts on the wing, 1 middle st, 128 sts on the wing, 3 border sts]

Cut Color A.

BORDER 1

With Color B, work 32 rows, following the Border 1 Chart (page 138) or the written instructions that follow. Then proceed to **Border 2** (page 136).

[327 sts: 3 border sts, 160 sts on the wing, 1 middle st, 160 sts on the wing, 3 border sts]

WRITTEN INSTRUCTIONS

Row 1 (RS): K3, (sm, yo, *p1, k1, yo, ssk, k8, k2tog, yo, k1, p1; work from * to m, yo, sm, k1) twice, k2. [4 sts inc'd]

Row 2 (WS): K3, (sm, k1, *k1, p3, k8, p3, k1; work from * to last st before m, k1, sm, k1) twice, k2.

Row 3: K3, (sm, yo, p1, *p1, k2, yo, ssk, k6, k2tog, yo, k2, p1; work from * to last st before m, p1, yo, sm, k1) twice, k2. [4 sts inc'd]

Row 4: K3, (sm, p1, k1, *k1, p4, k6, p4, k1; work from * to last 2 sts before m, k1, p1, sm, k1) twice, k2.

Row 5: K3, (sm, yo, k1, p1, *p1, k3, yo, ssk, k4, k2tog, yo, k3, p1; work from * to last 2 sts before m, p1, k1, yo, sm, k1) twice, k2. [4 sts inc'd]

Row 6: K3, (sm, p2, k1, *k1, p5, k4, p5, k1; work from * to last 3 sts before m, k1, p2, sm, k1) twice, k2.

Row 7: K3, (sm, yo, k2tog, yo, p1, *p1, [yo, ssk, k2] twice, k2tog, yo, k2, k2tog, yo, p1; work from * to last 3 sts before m, p1, yo, ssk, yo, sm, k1) twice, k2. [4 sts inc'd]

Row 8: K3, (sm, p2, k2, *[k2, p5] twice, k2; work from * to last sts 4 before m, k2, p2, sm, k1) twice, k2.

Row 9: K3, (sm, yo, k2tog, yo, p2, *p2, yo, ssk, k3, p2, k3, k2tog, yo, p2; work from * to last 4 sts before m, p2, yo, ssk, yo, sm, k1) twice, k2. [4 sts inc'd]

Row 10: K3, (sm, p2, k3, *k3, p4, k2, p4, k3; work from * to last 5 sts before m, k3, p2, sm, k1) twice, k2.

Row 11: K3, (sm, yo, k2tog, yo, p3, *p3, yo, ssk, k2, p2, k2, k2tog, yo, p3; work from * to last 5 sts before m, p3, yo, ssk, yo, sm, k1) twice, k2. [4 sts inc'd]

Row 12: K3, (sm, p2, k4, *k4, p3, k2, p3, k4; work from * to last 6 sts before m, k4, p2, sm, k1) twice, k2.

Row 13: K3, (sm, yo, k2tog, yo, p4, *p4, yo, ssk, k1, p2, k1, k2tog, yo, p4; work from * to last 6 sts before m, p4, yo, ssk, yo, sm, k1) twice, k2. [4 sts inc'd]

Row 14: K3, (sm, p2, k5, *k5, p2, k2, p2, k5; work from * to last 7 sts before m, k5, p2, sm, k1) twice, k2.

Row 15: K3, (sm, yo, k2, p5, *p5, 2/2/2 RPC, p5; work from * to last 7 sts before m, p5, k2, yo, sm, k1) twice, k2. [4 sts inc'd]

Row 16: K3, (sm, k1, p2, k5, *k5, p2, k2, p2, k5; work from * to last 8 sts before m, k5, p2, k1, sm, k1) twice, k2.

Row 17: K3, (sm, yo, p1, k1, yo, ssk, p4, *p4, k2tog, yo, k1, p2, k1, yo, ssk, p4; work from * to last 8 sts before m, p4, k2tog, yo, k1, p1, yo, sm, k1) twice, k2. [4 sts inc'd]

Row 18: K3, (sm, k2, p3, k4, *k4, p3, k2, p3, k4; work from * to last 9 sts before m, k4, p3, k2, sm, k1) twice, k2.

Row 19: K3, (sm, yo, p2, k2, yo, ssk, p3, *p3, k2tog, yo, k2, p2, k2, yo, ssk, p3; work from * to last 9 sts before m, p3, k2tog, yo, k2, p2, yo, sm, k1) twice, k2. [4 sts inc'd]

Row 20: K3, (sm, p1, k2, p4, k3, *k3, p4, k2, p4, k3; work from * to last 10 sts before m, k3, p4, k2, p1, sm, k1) twice, k2.

Row 21: K3, (sm, yo, k1, p2, k3, yo, ssk, p2, *p2, k2tog, yo, k3, p2, k3, yo, ssk, p2; work from * to last 10 sts before m, p2, k2tog, yo, k3, p2, k1, yo, sm, k1) twice, k2. [4 sts inc'd]

Row 22: K3, (sm, p2, k2, p5, k2, *[k2, p5] twice, k2; work from * to last 11 sts before m, k2, p5, k2, p2, sm, k1) twice, k2.

Row 23: K3, (sm, yo, k2tog, yo, p2, yo, ssk, k2, yo, ssk, p1, *p1, k2tog, yo, k2, k2tog, yo, p2, yo, ssk, k2, yo, ssk, p1; work from * to last 11 sts before m, p1, k2tog, yo, k2, k2tog, yo, p2, yo, ssk, yo, sm, k1) twice, k2. [4 sts inc'd]

Row 24: K3, (sm, p3, k2, p6, k1, *k1, p6, k2, p6, k1; work from * to last 12 sts before m, k1, p6, k2, p3, sm, k1) twice, k2.

Row 25: K3, (sm, yo, k2tog, yo, k1, p2, k1, yo, ssk, k3, p1, *p1, k3, k2tog, yo, k1, p2, k1, yo, ssk, k3, p1; work from * to last 12 sts before m, p1, k3, k2tog, yo, k1, p2, k1, yo, ssk, yo, sm, k1) twice, k2. [4 sts inc'd]

Row 26: K3, (sm, p4, k2, p6, k1, *k1, p6, k2, p6, k1; work from * to last 13 sts before m, k1, p6, k2, p4, sm, k1) twice, k2.

[continued]

Row 27: K3, [sm, (yo, k2tog) twice, yo, p2, (yo, ssk) twice, k2, p1, *p1, k2, (k2tog, yo) twice, p2, (yo, ssk) twice, k2, p1; work from * to last 13 sts before m, p1, k2, (k2tog, yo) twice, p2, (yo, ssk) twice, yo, sm, k1] twice, k2. [4 sts inc'd]

Row 28: K3, (sm, p5, k2, p6, k1, *k1, p6, k2, p6, k1; work from * to last 14 sts before m, k1, p6, k2, k5, sm, k1) twice, k2.

Row 29: K3, [sm, (yo, k2tog) twice, yo, k1, p2, k1, (yo, ssk) twice, k1, p1, *p1, k1, (k2tog, yo) twice, k1, p2, k1, (yo, ssk) twice, k1, p1; work from * to last 14 sts before m, p1, k1, (k2tog, yo) twice, k1, p2, k1, (yo, ssk) twice, yo, sm, k1] twice, k2. [4 sts inc'd]

Row 30: K3, (sm, p6, k2, p6, k1, *k1, p6, k2, p6, k1; work from * to last 15 sts before m, k1, p6, k2, p6, sm, k1) twice, k2.

Row 31: K3, [sm, (yo, k2tog) 3 times, yo, p2, (yo, ssk) 3 times, p1, *p1, (k2tog, yo) 3 times, p2, (yo, ssk) 3 times, p1; work from * to last 15 sts before m, p1, (k2tog, yo) 3 times, p2, (yo, ssk) 3 times, yo, sm, k1) twice, k2. [4 sts inc'd]

Row 32: K3, (sm, p7, k2, p6, k1, *k1, p6, k2, p6, k1; work from * to last 16 sts before m, k1, p6, k2, p7, sm, k1) twice, k2.

CHART INSTRUCTIONS

Starting at row 1 of Border 1 Chart (page 138) and working your way to the end of the chart, work all 32 rows the following way:

RS row: K3, sm, work from Border 1 Chart to next m, sm, k1, sm, work same row of chart to next m, sm, k3. [4 sts inc'd]

WS row: K3, sm, work from Border 1 Chart to next m, sm, k1, sm, work same row of chart to next m, sm, k3.

BORDER 2

With Color B, work 16 rows, following the Border 2 Charts (page 139) or the written instructions that follow. Then proceed to **Finishing** (page 137).

[647 sts: 3 border sts, 320 sts on the wing, 1 middle st, 320 sts on the wing, 3 border sts]

WRITTEN INSTRUCTIONS

Row 1 (RS): K3, sm, *p1, k1, (yo, k2tog) twice, yo, k1, p2, k1, (yo, ssk) twice, yo, k1, p1; repeat from * to m, sm, p1, sm, *p1, k1, (yo, k2tog) twice, yo, k1, p2, k1, (yo, ssk) twice, yo, k1, p1; repeat from * to marker, sm, k3. [2 sts inc'd per repeat]

Row 2 (WS): K3, sm, *k1, p7, k2, p7, k1; repeat from * to m, sm, k1, sm, *k1, p7, k2, p7, k1; repeat from * to marker, sm, k3.

Row 3: K3, sm, *p1, k1, (yo, k2tog) 3 times, yo, p2, (yo, ssk) 3 times, yo, k1, p1; repeat from * to m, sm, p1, sm, *p1, k1, (yo, k2tog) 3 times, yo, p2, (yo, ssk) 3 times, yo, k1, p1; repeat from * to marker, sm, k3. [2 sts inc'd per repeat]

Row 4: K3, sm, *k1, p8, k2, p8, k1; repeat from * to m, sm, k1, sm, *k1, p8, k2, p8, k1; repeat from * to m, sm, k3.

Row 5: K3, sm, *p1, k1, (yo, k2tog) 3 times, yo, k1, p2, k1, (yo, ssk) 3 times, yo, k1, p1; repeat from * to m, sm, p1, sm, *p1, k1, (yo, k2tog) 3 times, yo, k1, p2, k1, (yo, ssk) 3 times, yo, k1, p1; repeat from * to marker, sm, k3. [2 sts inc'd per repeat]

Row 6: K3, sm, *k1, p9, k2, p9, k1; repeat from * to m, sm, k1, sm, *k1, p9, k2, p9, k1; repeat from * to m, sm, k3.

Row 7: K3, sm, *p1, k1, (yo, k2tog) 4 times, yo, p2, (yo, ssk) 4 times, yo, k1, p1; repeat from * to m, sm, p1, sm, *p1, k1, (yo, k2tog) 4 times, yo, p2, (yo, ssk) 4 times, yo, k1, p1; repeat from * to m, sm, k3. [2 sts inc'd per repeat]

Row 8: K3, sm, *k1, p10, k2, p10, k1; repeat from * to m, sm, k1, sm, *p1, k1, (yo, k2tog) 4 times, yo, p2, (yo, ssk) 4 times, yo, k1, p1; repeat from * to m, sm, k3.

Row 9: K3, sm, *p1, k1, (yo, k2tog) 4 times, yo, k1, p2, k1, (yo, ssk) 4 times, yo, k1, p1; repeat from * to m, sm, p1, sm, *p1, k1, (yo, k2tog) 4 times, yo, k1, p2, k1, (yo, ssk) 4 times, yo, k1, p1; repeat from * to m, sm, k3. [2 sts inc'd per repeat]

Row 10: K3, sm, *k1, p11, k2, p11, k1; repeat from * to m, sm, k1, sm, *k1, p11, k2, p11, k1; repeat from * to m, sm, k3.

Row 11: K3, sm, *p1, k1, (yo, k2tog) 5 times, yo, p2, (yo, ssk) 5 times, yo, k1, p1; repeat from * to m, sm, p1, sm, *p1, k1, (yo, k2tog) 5 times, yo, p2, (yo, ssk) 5 times, yo, k1, p1; repeat from * to m, sm, k3. [2 sts inc'd per repeat]

Row 12: K3, sm, *k1, p12, k2, p12, k1; repeat from * to m, sm, k1, sm, *k1, p12, k2, p12, k1; repeat from * to m, sm, k3.

Row 13: K3, sm, *p1, k1, (yo, k2tog) 5 times, yo, k1, p2, k1, (yo, ssk) 5 times, yo, k1, p1; repeat from * to m, sm, p1, sm, *p1, k1, (yo, k2tog) 5 times, yo, k1, p2, k1, (yo, ssk) 5 times, yo, k1, p1; repeat from * to m, sm, k3. [2 sts inc'd per repeat]

Row 14: K3, sm, *k1, p13, k2, p13, k1; repeat from * to m, sm, k1, sm, *k1, p13, k2, p13, k1; repeat from * to m, sm, k3.

Row 15: K3, sm, *p1, k1, (yo, k2tog) 6 times, yo, p2, (yo, ssk) 6 times, yo, k1, p1; repeat from * to m, sm, p1, sm, *p1, k1, (yo, k2tog) 6 times, yo, p2, (yo, ssk) 6 times, yo, k1, p1; repeat from * to m, sm, k3. [2 sts inc'd per repeat]

Row 16: K3, sm, *k1, p14, k2, p14, k1; repeat from * to m, sm, k1, sm, *k1, p14, k2, p14, k1; repeat from * to m, sm, k3.

CHART INSTRUCTIONS

Starting at row 1 of the Border 2 Charts (page 139) and working your way to the end of the charts, work all 16 rows.

FINISHING

BO all sts knitwise.

Weave in all ends.

Block to the desired dimensions, placing pins at each purl stitch ridge to create a scalloped edge.

CHART KEY

□	RS: knit WS: purl
•	RS: purl WS: knit
O	yo
╲	ssk
╱	k2tog
⨵	2/2/2 RPC
□	repeat
▓	no stitch

[continued]

BORDER 1 CHART

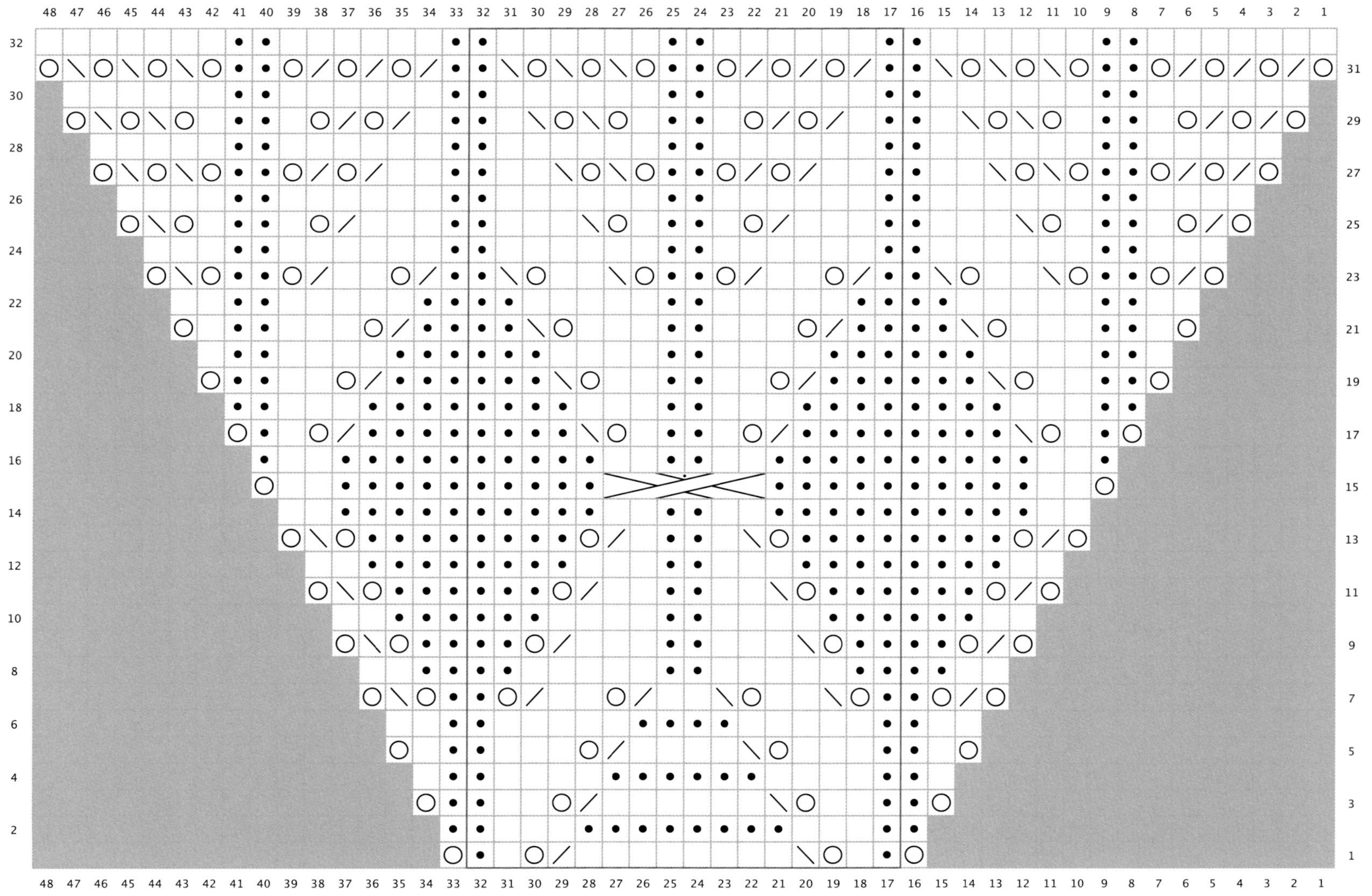

BORDER 2 CHART (RIGHT)

BORDER 2 CHART (LEFT)

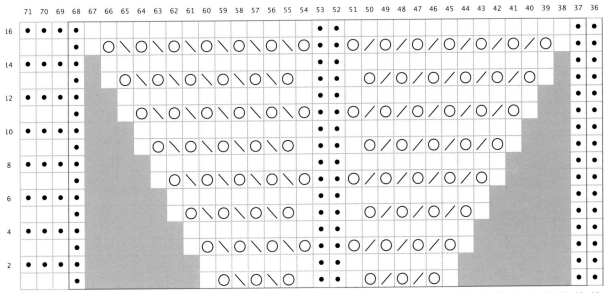

Filigree Scrunchie

This cute accessory will brighten your days and embellish your hair! The Filigree Scrunchie is an original way to use leftover yarns from other projects. It can be made with either one or two colors, and it requires very little yardage for instant knitting satisfaction. The seamless construction is sure to create a polished accessory that will add a romantic touch to your buns and ponytails.

Construction

The Filigree Scrunchie starts with a provisional cast-on. For the first few rounds, it is worked in stockinette stitch in the round to create a cover piece for an elastic hair tie. Once this piece is completed, the provisional cast-on is undone and placed on extra needles. The piece is turned upside down and the hair tie is placed in the middle. Both sides of live stitches are joined together, covering the hair tie. A lace frill is worked from those stitches. Once the first frill is completed, the stitches are picked up from the joining round and a second frill is worked.

Skill Level: Intermediate

Size

- One size (adaptable) to cover a hair tie with a 2-inch (5-cm) diameter

Materials

YARN
Fingering weight, Miss Babs Caroline (70% superwash merino wool; 20% cashmere; 10% nylon), 400 yds (365 m) per 95-g skein

YARDAGE / METERAGE
Color A: 33 yds (30 m)
Color B: 15 yds (14 m)

SHOWN IN
Color A: Rosy Finch (1 skein)
Color B: Dark Adobe (1 skein)
Any laceweight to DK weight yarn can be used for this pattern. Gauge, yardage and final size will vary. The scrunchie can also be made with only one color. Using leftover yarns is encouraged.

NEEDLES
Two sets of US 2 (2.75 mm), 12-inch (30-cm) or 12- to 24-inch (30- to 60-cm) circular needles

NOTIONS
1 stitch marker
Tapestry needle
Waste yarn
Elastic hair tie (2 inches [5 cm] in diameter or desired size)

(continued)

Gauge

28 sts × 32 rows = 4 inches (10 cm) in frill pattern (blocked)

32 sts × 40 rows = 4 inches (10 cm) in stockinette stitch (blocked)

Important note: Gauge isn't crucial for this pattern. Make sure to make the Hair Tie Cover to the correct dimensions to loosely encase your elastic hair tie.

Special Technique

Crochet Provisional Cast-On (page 150)

ABBREVIATIONS	
BO	bind off
CO	cast on
k	knit
k2tog	knit two together
p	purl
pm	place marker
prov CO	provisional cast-on
rnd(s)	round(s)
RS	right side
st(s)	stitch(es)
ssk	slip slip knit
WS	wrong side
yo	yarn over

Filigree Scrunchie Pattern

HAIR TIE COVER

With waste yarn, CO 52 sts, or any multiple of 4 sts, using the Crochet Provisional Cast-On.

Join working yarn (Color A).

K all sts, pm and join to work in the round.

K all sts for 9 more rnds or number of rnds required to cover your hair tie loosely when the work is folded in half.

Undo prov CO and place sts on second circular needle.

Turn your work inside out so the WS is facing you. Place your hair tie around the work, in the middle, and fold the work so both needles are at the top: the working needle with yarn attached in front, the needle with CO sts at the back. The RS is facing you, and the hair tie is inside.

Joining rnd: *K together 1 st from front needle and 1 st from back needle; repeat from * until all sts have been worked together. Only one circular needle remains.

Pm and join to work in the round.

FIRST FRILL

Work 8 rnds from Frill Chart (page 143) or the written instructions that follow.

Frill rnd 1: [P1, (yo, k1) 3 times, yo] around. [104 sts or twice your CO sts]

Frill rnd 2: P all sts.

Frill rnd 3: (P1, k7) around.

Frill rnd 4: [P1, k2tog, (yo, k1) 3 times, yo, ssk] around. [130 sts or 2.5 times your CO sts]

Frill rnd 5: P all sts.

Frill rnd 6: (P1, k9) around.

Frill rnd 7: [P1, k2tog, (k1, yo) 4 times, k1, ssk] around. [156 sts or 3 times your CO sts]

Frill rnd 8: P all sts.

BO all sts knitwise.

SECOND FRILL

Turn work so the joining rnd is on the purl side.

With Color B, pick up and k 48 sts in the purl bumps of the joining rnd.

Pm and join to work in the round.

Note that the frills' wrong sides are facing each other.

Work 8 rnds from the Frill Chart or the preceding written instructions.

BO all sts knitwise.

FINISHING

Weave in ends, wash and block frills.

CHART KEY

☐	knit
•	purl
O	yo
/	k2tog
\	ssk
▓	no stitch

FRILL CHART

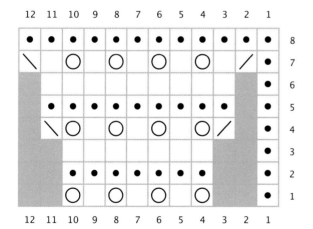

Meadow Socks

Meadows, those open areas where native plants freely grow under the sun, are inspiring in their natural simplicity. These socks are like a meadow, covered with unpretentious little flowers. They are arranged in tightly bound columns that create a lovely open texture. These socks are worked from the cuff down, allowing you to knit short cuffs for summer-perfect "sockettes" or longer ones for an all-year garment.

Construction

These socks are worked in the round from the cuff down, starting with a short ribbing section followed by the leg with texture all around. The top stitches are placed on hold and a square heel is then worked flat. The stitches on hold and the stitches along the edges are then picked up and worked in the round, while the lace pattern resumes over the sock. The foot is then worked, followed by the toes, which are grafted together to close the sock.

Skill Level: Intermediate

Sizes

- 1 (2)

Finished Measurements

- **Finished leg circumference:** 7.5 (9) inches / 19 (23) cm, blocked

Materials

YARN
Fingering weight, Sweet Paprika Designs Messa di Voce (100% superwash merino), 460 yds (420 m) per 100-g skein

YARDAGE/METERAGE
198 (305) yds / 181 (279) m

SHOWN IN
Cardamom (1 skein)

NEEDLES
For ribbing: US 0 (2 mm), DPNs or 32-inch (80-cm) circular needle for magic loop, or two circulars or 9-inch (23-cm) circular needle
For body of sock: US 2 (2.75 mm), DPNs or 32-inch (80-cm) circular needle for magic loop, or two circulars or 9-inch (23-cm) circular needle

NOTIONS
3 stitch markers
Tapestry needle

Gauge

32 sts × 44 rows = 4 inches (10 cm) in twisted ribbing (blocked), with smaller needles

32 sts × 44 rows = 4 inches (10 cm) in stockinette stitch and lace pattern (blocked), with larger needles

Special Techniques

German Twisted Cast-On (page 150)
Kitchener Stitch (page 153)

[continued]

ABBREVIATIONS	
BOR	beginning of round
CO	cast on
dec'd	decreased
k	knit
k2tog	knit two together
m	marker
m1r	make one right
p	purl
p2tog	purl two together
pm	place marker
rem	remaining
rnd(s)	round(s)
RS	right side
sl	slip
sm	slip marker
ssk	slip slip knit
sssk	slip slip slip knit
st(s)	stitch(es)
tbl	through back loop
WS	wrong side
wyib	with yarn in back
wyif	with yarn in front
yo	yarn over

Meadow Socks Pattern

Both socks are worked alike.

With smaller needles, using the German Twisted Cast-On, CO 60 (72) sts.

Pm and join to work in the round.

CUFF

Work in twisted ribbing for 0.75 inch / 2 cm, as follows:

Twisted ribbing: (K1 tbl, p1) around.

LEG

Switch to larger needles.

Work leg rnds 1–4 until leg measures approximately 2.5 (3) inches / 6.25 (7.5) cm or the desired length from cast-on edge, ending on leg rnd 2. Then proceed to **Heel Flap**.

Leg rnd 1: (K1 tbl, p1, yo, sssk, yo, p1) around.

Leg rnds 2–4: [K1 tbl, (p1, k1) twice, p1] around.

HEEL FLAP

Remove m and place first 30 (36) sts onto one needle. Heel will be worked back and forth in rows on these sts. The rem 30 (36) sts will be worked later for instep.

Heel flap row (RS): Sl1 wyib, k to end.

Heel flap row (WS): Sl1 wyif, p to end.

Work a total of 22 (30) heel flap rows.

HEEL TURN

Pm after the 10th (12th) st and after the 20th (24th) st.

Work short rows as follows:

Short row 1 (RS): Sl1 wyib, k to second m, sm, ssk, turn work.

Short row 2 (WS): Sl1 wyif, sm, p to m, sm, p2tog, turn work.

Repeat short rows 1–2 until all sts have been worked and 1 st remains on either side of the markers. [12 (14) sts remain]

Next row (RS): K all heel sts, removing markers.

GUSSET

Setup row: Pick up and k 12 (16) sts along the edge of heel flap, pm, [k1 tbl, (p1, k1) twice, p1] 5 (6) times, m1r, pm, pick up and k 12 (16) sts along heel flap, k 6 (7), pm to indicate BOR (located at center of heel). [67 (83) sts]

Start working in the round.

Work gusset rnds 1–4 for a total of 6 (10) rnds, ending with rnd 2. [61 (73) sts]. Then proceed to **Foot**.

Gusset rnd 1: K to m, sm, [k1 tbl, (p1, k1) twice, p1] 5 (6) times, k1 tbl, sm, k to end.

Gusset rnd 2: K to 3 sts before m, k2tog, k1, sm, (k1 tbl, p1, yo, sssk, yo, p1) 5 (6) times, k1 tbl, sm, k1, ssk, k to end. [2 sts dec'd]

Gusset rnd 3: Repeat rnd 1.

Gusset rnd 4: K to 3 sts before m, k2tog, k1, sm, [k1 tbl, (p1, k1) twice, p1] 5 (6) times, k1 tbl, sm, k1, ssk, k to end. [2 sts dec'd]

FOOT

Work foot rnds 1–4 until piece measures approximately 7 (9) inches / 18 (23) cm from back of heel or 2 (2.25) inches / 5 (5.5) cm less than the desired finished length, ending with foot rnd 4. Then proceed to **Shaping Toes**.

Foot rnd 1: K to m, sm, [k1 tbl, (p1, k1) twice, p1] 5 (6) times, k1 tbl, sm, k to end.

Foot rnd 2: Repeat rnd 1.

Foot rnd 3: K to m, sm, (k1 tbl, p1, yo, sssk, yo, p1) 5 (6) times, k1 tbl, sm, k to end.

Foot rnd 4: Repeat rnd 1.

SHAPING TOES

Toe rnd 1: (K to 3 sts before m, k2tog, k1, sm, k1, ssk) twice, k to end. [4 sts dec'd]

Toe rnd 2: K all sts.

Work toe rnds 1–2, 6 (8) times total [12 (16) rnds total]. [37 (41) sts]

Last toe rnd: K to 3 sts before m, k2tog, k1, sm, k1, ssk, k to 3 sts before m, k2tog, k1, sm, k1, ssk, k to end. [34 (38) sts]

Final rnd: K first 8 (9) sts only.

FINISHING

Cut yarn, leaving a 12-inch (30-cm) tail.

Place first 17 (19) sts on one needle and last 17 (19) sts on a second needle. Use the Kitchener stitch to graft toe sts.

Weave in all ends. Block to the desired dimensions.

Stitch Tutorials

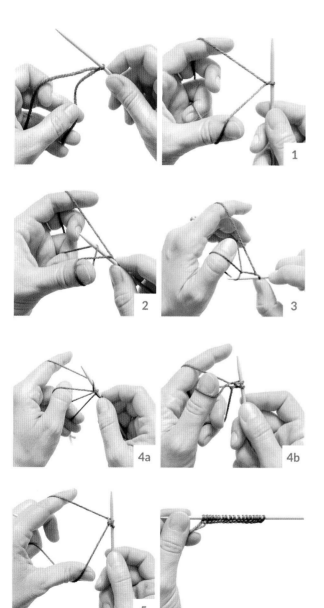

German Twisted Cast-On

The German twisted cast-on is an excellent technique for casting on stitches for an edge that requires some stretchiness; for example, around the neck for a top-down sweater, around the head for a hat or around the leg for cuff-down socks. This technique is a stretchier version of the long-tail cast-on.

MATERIALS

- Working yarn
- Working needles

TUTORIAL

Preparation step: Make a slipknot, leaving a long tail of yarn, and place it on the needle.

Step 1: Hold the yarn in a slingshot position, with the long tail looping around the thumb and the working yarn around the pointing finger, holding both strands of yarn with your other fingers.

Step 2: Place the needle above the work, close to your body, and pass it under both strands of yarn wrapped around your thumb.

Step 3: With your needle, catch the thumb strand that is farthest away from you and bring it under the other thumb strand, forming a small loop on the needle.

Step 4: Catch the finger strand by passing the needle above it and then below, and pass the strand through the loop on the needle.

Step 5: Drop the yarn from your thumb and tighten the stitch by pulling on the strand with your thumb, returning your hand to the slingshot position.

Repeat steps 1–5 until you have cast on the desired number of stitches.

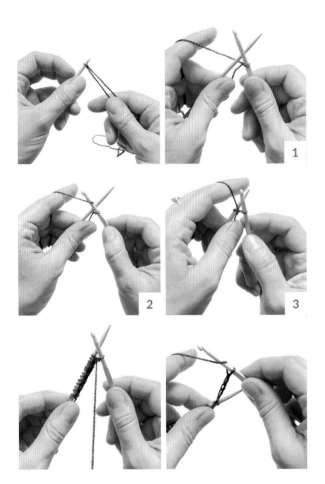

Crochet Provisional Cast-On

The provisional cast-on is an essential technique that enables a whole panoply of knitting constructions. When working from this cast-on, you can easily pick up stitches back at the cast-on edge and seamlessly work the other way. In this book, this technique is used to knit a double-layer brim on the Feather Hat (page 45) and to work the collar of the Amarelle Sweater (page 85) after working the body, for a close and comfortable fit. There are several ways to work a provisional cast-on. My favorite technique is this one, worked with a crochet hook and some waste yarn.

MATERIALS

- Waste yarn (similar size to your working yarn)
- Crochet hook (similar or smaller size to your working needles)
- Working needles
- Working yarn

TUTORIAL

CASTING ON

Preparation step: With waste yarn, make a slipknot and place it on the crochet hook.

Step 1: Holding the crochet hook in your right hand, crossed over the needle held in your left hand, place the yarn on the back of the needle.

Step 2: Wrap the yarn over the crochet hook.

Step 3: Draw the yarn through the loop on the crochet hook.

Repeat steps 1–3 until you have cast on the desired number of stitches.

Final step: Chain a few stitches and cut the yarn, passing the end through the last stitch.

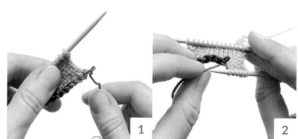

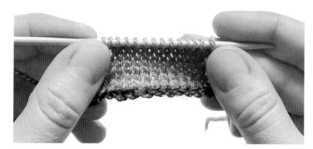

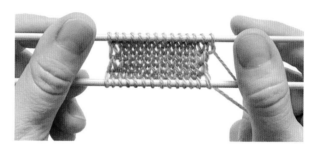

USING WORKING YARN

Join your working yarn, and work through all the stitches of the cast-on as the pattern calls for.

Follow the pattern to complete the work until instructed to undo the provisional cast-on.

UNDOING THE PROVISIONAL CAST-ON

Preparation step: Undo the end of the chained stitches and pull the yarn to unzip the chain.

Step 1: Pull the yarn to unzip one stitch of the provisional cast-on.

Step 2: Place the stitch on the needle.

Repeat steps 1–2 until the cast-on has been completely undone and all stitches are on a live needle.

Bobbles

Bobbles are a sweet way to embellish lace patterns. There are numerous ways of making them, all of which can seem difficult or intimidating. Over the years, I refined my technique to adopt this one, which is the easiest for me–and many knitters have told me they finally enjoy working bobbles since learning this technique! I'm not going to say that these bobbles are easy to make, but with a bit of practice, this technique can become a good solution for those who hate making bobbles but who love how they look. Note that in all the patterns made with bobbles, you can also decide to omit them, and you'll still be making some lovely lacework.

MATERIALS

- Working yarn
- Working needles
- A crochet hook smaller that your knitting needles

TUTORIAL

Preparation step: Work up to the stitch where the bobble will be made.

Step 1: Pick up the crochet hook. With the yarn in back, insert the crochet hook knitwise in the next stitch and pull up a loop.

Step 2: Yarn over the crochet hook.

Work steps 1–2 five times, total (see Note). [10 loops on crochet hook]

Step 3: Pull the last yarn over through all the other stitches on the crochet hook. [1 loop on crochet hook]

Step 4: Insert the crochet hook under the bar of the stitch made at the previous row. [2 loops on crochet hook]

Step 5: Yarn over and pull through both loops on the crochet hook.

Step 6: Place the stitch from the crochet hook on the right-hand needle.

- -

Note: You can work a different number of repetitions if you'd like. I recommend making a swatch to see the result with your personal tension. In general, I like to make 5 repetitions with fingering weight yarn, 4 repetitions with DK weight yarn and 3 repetitions with worsted weight yarn.

- -

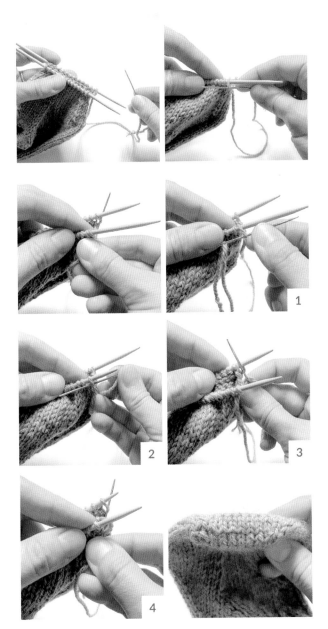

Kitchener Stitch

The Kitchener stitch is used to join two sets of live stitches together while also perfectly reproducing the look of knit stitches. It is used instead of sewing bound-off edges together, resulting in a finished look without a bulky seam.

MATERIALS

- Working yarn
- Tapestry needle
- Working needles

Note: With socks, the stitches are equally split onto two needles, with the top stitches on one needle and the bottom stitches on the other. The working yarn should be cut from the ball, with a long tail that is 20 inches (51 cm) long.

TUTORIAL

Preparation step 1: Thread the yarn through the tapestry needle. Place the needle with the top stitches in front and the needle with the bottom stitches in back. Insert the tapestry needle from back to front (purlwise) into the first stitch on the front needle. Draw the yarn all the way through and leave the stitch on the needle.

Preparation step 2: Insert the needle from front to back (knitwise) into the first stitch on the back needle. Draw the yarn all the way through and leave the stitch on the needle.

Step 1: Insert the needle **knitwise** into the first stitch on the front needle, draw the yarn through and **drop** the stitch from the needle.

Step 2: Insert the needle **purlwise** into the next stitch on the **front** needle, draw the yarn through and **keep** the stitch on the needle.

Step 3: Insert the needle **purlwise** into the first stitch on the **back** needle, draw the yarn through and **drop** the stitch from the needle.

Step 4: Insert the needle **knitwise** into the next stitch on the **back** needle, draw the yarn through and **keep** the stitch on the needle.

Repeat steps 1–4 until only one stitch is left on each needle.

Work steps 1 and 3 on these stitches.

153

Acknowledgments

First and foremost, I want to thank my mom, Loraine Vadnais, and my life partner, Robert Tétreault, who both have actively participated in the creation of this book so much that I consider this **our** work, **our** book.

My mom, in addition to her unconditional love and support, knitted several samples, entirely or in part, with an uncommon dedication. Any sea of stockinette or garter stitch that you can see in this book, as well as some of the lace, has been kindly knitted by her hands. She even knitted the bottom part of the Pinnate Tank Top in one day, from five in the morning to nine at night, because the next day was my only chance at taking pictures among the blooming apple trees. I'm thankful that we have such similar knitting tensions that we can switch in the middle of a project. And I'm even more thankful for having been raised by this incredible woman with her positive energy!

Robert encouraged me in this project and believed in me from the start of my designing journey. After learning to be a photographer just so that he could take pictures of my patterns a few years ago, he took all the photos in this book in a way that I couldn't imagine was possible, which shows how talented he is. He also took care of our kids when I needed extra working time, cooked most of our meals and cleaned our home while I was knitting—all on top of his own professional life. He's an amazing man and father. Day after day, he committed to bringing my dream to reality.

I also want to thank my dad, Denis Vézina, who was so proud of his daughter for following in his authorial footsteps and who gave me so much wise advice during the project—and so much more throughout my life!

I am indebted to my friend Carole Ann Armstrong, who's been cheering for me from day one.

I want to thank my kids for being so sweet, kind and caring and for being a constant source of joy and inspiration.

These people, **my** people, gave me so much support, so much love—they made me believe in myself.

This book wouldn't have been as inspiring if it weren't for the people who promptly and happily provided yarn in order for me to knit the samples. I am incredibly thankful for these professionals of the fiber industry who trusted me and this project:

- Lucinda Iglesias, store owner at Mont Tricot (Cedar Hat; Cedar Mittens)

- Naomi Endicott and Stephanie Earp, store owners at Espace Tricot (Amarelle Sweater)

- Julie Asselin, indie yarn dyer at Julie Asselin Yarns (Periwinkle Shawl)

- Amélie P. Bédard, indie yarn dyer at Émilia & Philomène (Pinnate Tank Top)

- Helen Cosgrove-Davies, yarn wrangler at Miss Babs Hand-Dyed Yarns and Fibers (Soft Breeze Shawl; Filigree Scrunchie)

- Elizabeth and Debbie Sullivan, indie yarn dyers and owners at Sweet Paprika Designs (Meadow Socks)

Of course, this book wouldn't have been possible without the tireless work of the dynamic team at Page Street. I am so grateful that Emily Taylor, my super editor, reached out to me with this project and gave me her trust, her precious support and her thoughtful advice at every single step. I also want to say thank you to Cathy Susko, who did an amazing work tech editing the patterns and who carefully worked on improving their readability and consistency while catching my typos and miscalculations. Many thanks to Laura Benton and Meg Baskis, who used some sort of magic and impressive designing skills to turn my long manuscript into a whimsical book that is perfectly in tone with the designs. Thanks to Meg Palmer, who took the time to kindly answer my multiple questions regarding the legal parts of the project. And I also want to thank everyone at Page Street who worked on this book and added their individual touches to the process of making this book come to life.

Over the years, an impressive number of knitters from all around the world have helped me push my patterns one step forward by testing them and giving me their sincere opinions. I learned **a lot** from them, from their diverse knitting journeys and from their countless years of cumulative knitting experience. I am grateful for every person on this loyal team of test knitters of more than 200 people! A smaller team worked with me on the patterns of the book, and I want to say thank you from the bottom of my heart to Mirva, Dee-Anne, Jayin, Myriam, Marianne, Paule, Nikki, Sarah, Mireille, Kim, Caroline, Sue, Rosalyn, Robin, Su Yan, Jessica, Kimmy, Brandy and Tiffany.

Lastly, I want to thank the members of the beautiful knitting community who have been supporting me for years and who have made my lifestyle possible. Thank you for letting me share my passion with you, and thank you for sharing yours with me. The pieces you create from my patterns are my ultimate recognition, the meaning behind my work. My deepest wish is to accompany you in your knitting journey for many years to come and to bring you joy with my patterns.

About the Author

Gabrielle Vézina is the knitwear designer behind Gabrielle Knits. Her cozy and elegant lace designs are enjoyed by knitters of all skill levels for their clear instructions and gratifying results. Gabrielle's patterns have been featured in various Knit Picks publications, *Interweave Knits* magazine and *Jane Austen Knits*, among others. She lives in Montréal, Canada, with her partner and two children.

Index

Index